Introducing
Glory to God

Introducing
Glory to God

A Guide for Welcoming the New Hymnal into Your Congregation

Edited by
Mary Louise Bringle

Geneva Press
Louisville, Kentucky

© 2014 Geneva Press

Portions of this book were previously published as downloadable studies on the Presbyterian Leader, www.ThePresbyterianLeader.com.

First edition
Published by Geneva Press
Louisville, Kentucky

14 15 16 17 18 19 20 21 22 23—10 9 8 7 6 5 4 3 2 1

All rights reserved. No part of this book may be reproduced or transmitted in any form or by any means, electronic or mechanical, including photocopying, recording, or by any information storage or retrieval system, without permission in writing from the publisher. For information, address Geneva Press, 100 Witherspoon Street, Louisville, Kentucky 40202-1396. Or contact us online at www.genevapress.com.

Book design by Erika Lundbom
Cover design by Lisa Buckley and Dilu Nicholas

Library of Congress Cataloging-in-Publication Data

Introducing Glory to God : a guide for welcoming the new hymnal into your congregation / edited by Mary Louise Bringle. -- First edition.
    pages cm
"Portions of this book were previously published as downloadable studies on the PresbyterianLeader, www.ThePresbyterianLeader.com."
    ISBN 978-0-664-50343-7 (pbk : alk. paper) 1. Presbyterian Church (U.S.A.)--Hymns--History and criticism. 2. Hymns--United States--History and criticism. 3. Glory to God. I. Bringle, Mary Louise.
ML3176.I57 2014
782.27088'285137--dc23

2014016581

∞The paper used in this publication meets the minimum requirements of the American National Standard for Information Sciences—Permanence of Paper for Printed Library Materials, ANSI Z39.48-1992.

Most Geneva Press books are available at special
quantity discounts when purchased in bulk by corporations,
organizations, and special-interest groups. For more information,
please e-mail SpecialSales@GenevaPress.com.

CONTENTS

Acknowledgments vii
Introduction ix

1. Why Another New Hymnal? 1
2. Challenges of Creating a New Hymnal 11
3. The Theology of *Glory to God* 21
4. Teachings on Salvation in *Glory to God* 31
5. Theological Vision Statement 41
6. Liturgy in *Glory to God* 45
7. Decisions about Language in *Glory to God* 60
8. A Statement on Language 71
9. Musical Genres in *Glory to God* 76
10. Introducing *Glory to God* to Your Church 89

Appendix 1: Fifteen Facts about Glory to God 99
Appendix 2: Suggested Uses for Old Hymnals 105

ACKNOWLEDGMENTS

Chapters 5 and 8 were written by the Presbyterian Committee on Congregational Song.

Chapter 6 was written by David Gambrell, who is Associate for Worship in the Presbyterian Church (U.S.A.) Office of Theology and Worship and a member of the Presbyterian Committee on Congregational Song.

Chapter 9 was written by Beverly A. Howard, who is a professor of music at California Baptist University and a member of the Presbyterian Committee on Congregational Song.

All other material was written by Mary Louise Bringle, who is professor of philosophy and religious studies at Brevard College in Brevard, North Carolina, and chair of the Presbyterian Committee on Congregational Song.

INTRODUCTION

If you open the cover of a hymnal and hold the book up to your ear, what do you hear? Literally, of course, the answer is nothing. The black dots and squiggles on the page, whether they signify music notes or words, do not take on the life for which they were intended until they are given breath and voice. A hymn is not really a hymn until it is sung by the people of God; a hymnal is not really a hymnal until it is used in worship for praise and lament, confession and adoration.

Yet, in a metaphorical sense, a lot can be heard from the pages of a hymnal. The voices of our families of faith come pouring out to us as we glimpse titles that remind us of people in whose presence we learned particular songs: parents and grandparents, Sunday school teachers, choir directors, youth leaders, friends gathered under a starry sky on a distant night at summer camp. We hear phrases that resonate in deep places within us: "Amazing Grace"; "Rock of Ages"; "Here I Am, Lord"; "Holy, Holy, Holy!" We sense the joys and struggles of psalm singers from ancient Israel, monks and nuns from medieval Europe, Protestant Reformers, African American slaves, Victorian women, twentieth-century revivalists, and twenty-first-century musicians keeping an old, old story fresh for new generations.

Still, there are many things we do not customarily hear, either literally or metaphorically, when we open our hymnals for use. We do not hear the forty-five minute debate in a hymnal committee about whether a particular text displays Trinitarian orthodoxy or heresy. We do not hear the hours of discussion about whether pronouns referring to God should be printed with capital or lowercase letters, in archaic (thee, thy) or contemporary (you, your) form. We do not hear the days spent by subcommittees going through every poetic text, line by line, to determine the best possible version from the many alternatives available across denominations and centuries of use or the many hours spent checking every tune, note by note, to arrive at a consensus regarding the most accessible key for singing and the optimal harmonization or accompaniment.

The creation of a hymnal involves thousands of such discussions on matters both large and seemingly small. Should the accompaniment for each piece be printed in the pew edition, requiring sometimes three or more pages for a single song and thereby cutting down on the number of selections that can be incorporated or should the keyboard parts be reserved for a separate edition for organists and pianists, meaning that the congregation's book cannot just be carried from pew to piano for accompanying every song? Should names of authors and composers go at the top of the page or the bottom—or be left off the page altogether (as was done in historic hymnals) and only mentioned in indexes at the back? Should a comma go between main clauses of a text (as has been the practice in Great Britain) or a semicolon (as is the standard practice in the United States)?

People who use congregational song collections are generally spared such minutiae and simply live with the decisions of editorial committees—often without even realizing that such matters had to be taken into consideration. Making a hymnal is not quite like making sausage: the behind-the-scenes activities are, for the most part, neither messy nor unsavory. However, they are meticulous and time-consuming. And they are largely hidden from view, not because of any desire to conceal, but because the purpose of the finished product is to praise God, not to bless or blame any human intermediaries.

The essays in this volume offer a peek into some of the processes by which *Glory to God* came into being: its organizational framework, language, music, liturgy, and theology. Reading through these articles, whether alone or as part of a study group, provides answers to an array of "what," "who," "how," and "why" questions about the new congregational song resource, which is, in fact, more than just a "hymnal" because it contains psalms and spiritual songs, not just hymns. (Look for this distinction in chapter 1.)

Whether hymns, psalms, or spiritual songs, worshipers often experience a deeper connection to the music they sing when they know more of the backstory of the individual pieces. From what country does this song come, and how does it enliven worship in its home culture? What circumstances in the text writer's life inspired the poem? What passages of Scripture are woven into the words? Why did the composer select a particular name for a particular tune? When and why was this tune married to this text? Topics like these are treated in miniature in the notes at the bottom of each selection in *Glory to God* (with the exception of the "Service Music," numbers 551 to 609). Such topics are treated in even greater detail in the hymnal companion, prepared to accompany *Glory to God* by hymnological scholar Carl P. Daw, himself a hymn writer of international renown (author of more than a dozen texts in *Glory to God*, including "Like the Murmur of the Dove's Song," "O Day of Peace," and a translation of Philip Nicolai's splendid Advent hymn, "'Sleepers, Wake!' A Voice Astounds Us").

With the present collection of essays, worshipers will have the opportunity to enjoy a deeper connection with the hymnal itself, gaining intimate insights into what went on during the years of committee deliberations and editorial decisions leading to the finished product. After reading these articles, people who open the covers of *Glory to God* and hold the book to their ears should be able to hear the members of the Presbyterian Committee on Congregational Song engaged in exchanging hymnological research, sharing heartfelt prayers, and arguing passionately (though never impolitely) about matters of theology and language; laughing and occasionally weeping together; shuffling thousands of papers; tapping on dozens of cell phones and laptops; and, above all, singing, always singing.

Mary Louise Bringle
Chair, Presbyterian Committee on Congregational Song

Chapter 1

WHY ANOTHER NEW HYMNAL?

Can you finish the lines of these hymns?

- Then sings my soul, my Savior, God, to Thee, _____
- God of the sparrow, God of _____
- Let us talents and _____
- Lift high _____
- Here I am, Lord. Is it I, Lord? _____

When asked, many Presbyterians know not just one following word but a whole series of phrases. In the last example, indeed, many can unhesitatingly sing the entire refrain by heart.

What is so remarkable about this? All five of the hymns in question were unfamiliar to Presbyterian congregations when the "new blue" hymnal appeared in 1990. Had churches never adopted that resource, these five songs—and many others just as meaningful and memorable—would have remained outside the shared worship life of Presbyterian Church (U.S.A.) congregations.

Instead, though, within a matter of a relatively few years, those once "new" songs became "old" favorites. "New" must, however, appear in quotation marks—these hymns were not all of recent vintage when they were selected for the 1990 hymnal. "Lift High the Cross," sung to the tune CRUCIFER, dates to 1916, and the English translation of "How Great Thou Art," to 1953. But these hymns had not appeared in earlier Presbyterian publications, so in the 1990s they were "new" to a particular group of people.

By the same token, "old" must also be qualified. When people say they love "the good old hymns," they generally do not mean the third-century Greek lamp-lighting hymn (the *Phos hilaron,* translated into such English versions as "O Gladsome Light"), or the fourth-century Latin texts of Bishop Ambrose of Milan (like "O Splendor of God's Glory Bright"). In fact, they often have in mind something of comparatively recent historical origin. In their minds, therefore, "old" does not so much mean "ancient" as it means often-used, comfortably familiar, or rich with personal associations. An "old hymn" is a bit like an old shoe: no matter how recently it was acquired, it is cherished in large part because it does not chafe or call attention to itself; rather, it simply helps to take us where we need to go—particularly, in the instance of a hymn, if we need to go into the presence of the living God.

THE ONGOING WORK OF THE SPIRIT

Efforts to identify and define "new" and "old" hymns show that songs currently unknown to a group of worshipers can, within the next several years, rise to the status of "old favorites"—"heart songs," songs that touch us deeply and help us experience more of who God is and what God would have us become. If we believe, as we profess in the Presbyterian Brief Statement of Faith, that "the same Spirit who inspired the prophets and apostles rules *our* faith and life," then surely we should leave the way open for that Spirit to continue inspiring people to craft songs expressive of each generation's distinctive challenges and joys.

Ultimately, one of the most important reasons for producing new hymnals is to provide access to this ongoing inspiration. Over the last decades of the twentieth century and the first decades of the twenty-first century, the field of church music has witnessed an unprecedented outpouring of creativity. Experts refer to a "hymn explosion" that began in Great Britain in the 1960s and has continued unabated since that time, expanding to the United States and numerous other countries. In fact, since the World Council of Churches met in Canberra, Australia, in 1991 (the year after the "blue" Presbyterian hymnal was published), tunes and texts from all around the globe have become available for widespread use as never before.

> . . . the field of church music has witnessed an unprecedented outpouring of creativity.

In addition to this exponential increase in works composed in the traditional "hymn" genre—a series of stanzas, all sung to the same tune, developing a theological theme or biblical narrative—the past generation has also witnessed an upsurge in what is variously referred to as "praise and worship" or "contemporary Christian" music. In contrast to hymns, this alternative genre sometimes assumes popular song form, with verses, a refrain, and a bridge; sometimes it takes the shape of a single chorus sung repeatedly to create a particular worshipful mood like exuberant joy or contemplative peace. Because of this repetitive structure, songs in the "praise chorus" repertoire, whether hailing from the United States or elsewhere, have sometimes been caricatured as "7/11 songs": seven words, sung eleven times over.

But any genre can be parodied: one could just as easily (and inaccurately) characterize traditional hymns as "11/7 songs": eleven-stanza treatises sung out of seven-pound books! The fact of the matter is that many moving and powerful worship songs do simply use the same words over and over. Think of the hymns "Come, Bring Your Burdens to God" or "Jesus, Remember Me, When You Come into Your Kingdom." On the other hand, numerous meaningful hymns require multiple stanzas to develop their ideas. These include Trinitarian hymns that have a stanza for each person of the Godhead, plus a final doxology celebrating their unity, or carols that unfold the whole drama of Jesus' life, death, and resurrection (like Sydney Carter's "The Lord of the Dance"). Both genres, the hymn and the praise song, can be done well or poorly; a principle of charity urges us to look for the best rather than the worst each has to offer.

THE GENERATIONAL WORK OF HYMNAL COMMITTEES

A hymnal committee must take this principle of charity to heart as it scans the immense spectrum of hymns that has become available to the church in recent years. Because of the abundance of hymns that exist today, denominations wanting access to the best of the new creations have had to form committees whose primary assignment is to "test the spirits" (1 John 4:1). Not every new song—or *old* song, for that matter—teaches sound doctrine or conveys its message through poetry and music suitable for giving glory to God. To survey the vast array of "hymns, psalms, and spiritual songs" (as Paul's letters inclusively referred to the variety of church music available to the churches of *his* day [Eph. 5:19; Col. 3:16]), groups with expertise in theology, music, and poetry are charged with the arduous process of selection.

Denominations and publishing houses convene such groups on a roughly *generational* basis. Anthropologists, genealogists, and biologists provide slightly different definitions of what counts as a "generation," but the average length rests somewhere between twenty and twenty-five years. This figure seems right for hymnologists as well. Roughly every two decades church groups look back over their song collections, winnowing out those older pieces that have fallen out of common usage and those newer ones that have never quite caught on. Such winnowing makes room for a new hymnal edition to add material created or discovered since the last time such revisions occurred. The Presbyterian Church U.S.A. is no exception to this two-decade cycle, although the pattern is slightly obscured because many churches did not adopt the *Worship Book* that came out in the 1970s, in between the "red" hymnbook of the 1950s and the "blue" hymnal of 1990.

Indeed, Presbyterians are in good company in undergoing a recent generational review process. Over the first decades of the twenty-first century, multiple denominations around the United States and abroad produced new song collections. In 2005, the Church of Scotland came out with *Church Hymnary IV*. In 2006, both Missouri Synod Lutherans and the Evangelical Lutheran Church in America brought out new worship resources (the *Lutheran Service Book* and *Evangelical Lutheran Worship*, respectively). The Southern Baptist convention in 2008 published the *Baptist Hymnal*, whose title deliberately omitted the definite article to acknowledge that another group of Baptists was at the same time creating *Celebrating Grace* (Mercer University Press, 2010). Responding to a Vatican-mandated new English translation of the liturgy, Roman Catholic publishing house GIA issued both *Gather III* and *Worship IV* in 2011. The banner year of 2013 projected the collaborative volume of the Christian Reformed Church and Reformed

Church in America, *Lift Up Your Hearts*; *Glory to God* from the Presbyterian Church (U.S.A.); and *Community of Christ Sings* from the Community of Christ (which changed its name in 2000 from the Reorganized Church of Jesus Christ of Latter Day Saints).

A pair of examples helps illustrate why hymn collections benefit from regular processes to (so to speak) wring out the old and ring in the new. Our grandparents or great-grandparents, had they been Presbyterian in either the northern or the southern church, would have likely been familiar with a hymn written by Horatius Bonar, poet and pastor of the Free Church of Scotland, "A Few More Years Shall Roll." This text appeared regularly—in the hymnals of 1874, 1895, 1901, and 1911—before it disappeared from denominational use. Its lyrics call attention to the short time remaining between any of us who are now alive and the day of our inevitable death:

> A few more years shall roll,
> a few more seasons come,
> and we shall be with those that rest
> asleep within the tomb. . . .
>
> A few more suns shall set
> o'er these dark hills of time,
> and we shall be where suns are not,
> a far serener clime. . . .

The poetry, which continues for another three stanzas, is vivid and artful, but it sounds slightly dated now. The word "clime" is no longer in use, even by hymn poets who need a good rhyming option. The image of "dark hills of time" seems to characterize the present world as exclusively a vale of tears and not also a gift of grace and arena for stewardship and mission. The yearning for "serener" company with those "asleep within the tomb" carries almost maudlin connotations to a twenty-first century ear (or even, apparently, to hymnal committees since the first decade of the twentieth century).

Contrast to this another hymn by the same author. The moving communion text, "Here, O My Lord, I See Thee Face to Face," has appeared in some version in every Presbyterian hymnal since 1895. Sometimes the language is pluralized ("Here, O *our* Lord") to make the hymn sound more like the song of a community receiving the Lord's Supper together than that of an individual partaking alone. Sometimes the pronouns for God are modernized ("we see *you* face to face") rather than preserved in the "thee/thou" form of Bonar's 1855 composition. Never are all eight of the text's original stanzas included—sometimes only four appear; the Presbyterian hymnals of 1895 and of 1990 both use five stanzas, but a different selection of five. *Glory to God* (2013) follows the pattern of its most immediate predecessor: first-person plural pronouns for humanity ("our/we"), "you/your" pronouns for God, and the same five stanzas as the 1990 hymnal, in the same order.

Such examples of wringing out and ringing in could be multiplied many times over, but the point is sufficiently clear: each generation puts its own stamp onto the hymns it selects for its hymnals. An outgrowth of this generational practice is the tendency of each individual singer to assume that whatever version she or he grew up singing is "the original," and everything else is a corruption. Such assumptions make intuitive sense—after all, the words and music we learned as children and young adults *are* "original" *for us*. In like manner, if we grew up with capital letters for pronouns referring to God, or with an Amen to conclude every hymn, we assume that such features have *always* been parts of proper hymnody, although in reality, they have not.

WHAT STAYS? WHAT GOES?

Times change, and trends in hymnody along with them. Over the century and a half since Presbyterians began singing hymns "of human composure" in worship and not just metered, rhyming versions of the divinely inspired Psalms of David, numerous texts and tunes—like "A Few More Years Shall Roll"—have come *and gone*. We have wrung out the old in eliminating such once-valued songs as "Ah! Wretched, Vile, Ungrateful Heart"; "How Condescending and How Kind Was God's Eternal Son"; and "Quiet, Lord, My Froward Heart" ("fro-ward," the opposite of "to-ward," once meant something along the lines of "perverse" or turned away from God). Typically, in fact, about half of the contents of one hymnal go by the wayside when its successor comes onto the scene.

> Typically, in fact, about half of the contents of one hymnal go by the wayside when its successor comes onto the scene.

But by the same token, about half of the contents remain. Numerous texts and tunes have also come *and stayed*, gaining such long-lived popularity that since the date of their introduction they have appeared in every subsequent denominational collection of worship songs. "Beneath the Cross of Jesus" cannot be found in the 1874 Presbyterian hymnal, but once it came to light in 1895, it became a constant companion. "O Beautiful for Spacious Skies" made its debut in the 1927 hymnal of the southern Presbyterian church and "Be Thou My Vision," in the northern church's hymnal of 1933; we would be unlikely now to have a hymnal without either. "God of Grace and God of Glory" and "I Greet Thee Who My Sure Redeemer Art" made their initial appearances in 1955; "Go Tell It on the Mountain" and "Lord of the Dance," in 1975;

"Here I Am, Lord" and the other examples from the introductory exercise were "new" to Presbyterians in 1990 but are already showing signs of longevity.

We do well to remind ourselves that *every* hymn was "new" once upon a time; were it not for regular hymnal revisions, our congregations would not have access to such new songs to sing. Our Sunday morning worship would still resound with strains of "Stay, Thou Insulted Spirit, Stay" from the hymnal of 1874, and not "Spirit of the Living God, Fall Afresh on Me," which was not written until 1935 and not included in a Presbyterian hymnal until 1990. Or perhaps, instead, without a steady cycle of rejuvenation, the singing of hymns would have narrowed to a smaller and smaller number of eighteenth- and nineteenth-century favorites until even these classics fell victim to the tedium of overuse.

Who among us, then, would presume to "quench the Spirit" (1 Thess. 5:19), bolting sanctuary doors against fresh inspiration under the assumption that the old hymns and songs are all we need? The psalmist repeatedly commands us to sing to the Lord a *new* song (Pss. 33, 40, 96, 98, 144, 149), understanding that our worship can only thus remain faithful to a God who is perennially doing "a new thing" (Isa. 43:19). Every twenty years or so, a church has the opportunity and privilege of reexamining its repertoire of song, making prayerful decisions about what has worn well, what has worn out, and what might wear like a well-crafted and comfortable shoe, carrying current and future generations into the presence of the living God.

Like our parents, grandparents, and great-grandparents who lived to see the advent of new hymnals in 1990, 1975, 1955, 1933, and on back into historical memory, we can face such times of transition with eagerness and confidence. We can do so because we firmly believe, to cite again A Brief Statement of Faith, that "the same Spirit who inspired the prophets and apostles" continues to "rule our life and faith." Or, to borrow words from the opening stanza of a hymn that has surely stood the test of time, appearing in some version in every Presbyterian hymnal since 1874 (#687 in *Glory to God*), we trust that the God who has been "our help in ages past" will remain "our hope for years to come."

Chapter 2

CHALLENGES OF CREATING A NEW HYMNAL

"The church of Christ in every age, beset by change but Spirit-led, must claim and test its heritage."

—Fred Pratt Green, "The Church of Christ in Every Age"

How many Presbyterians does it take to change a hymnal? A classic light bulb joke answer springs to mind: "Change?! Who said anything about change?!" But perhaps we can be more precise than that. At the local church level, we might answer something like: Seventeen: *one* worship planner excited about the possibility of choosing new songs for worship that aren't available in the current hymnal; *five* members of a music committee who hear about the new hymnal from this worship planner and investigate the possibility of using it in their congregation; *nine* members of a session who act on the report of the committee; *one* administrative assistant who places an order with the publishing house; and *one* church treasurer who cuts a check in the appropriate amount.

Or, speaking nationally, we might instead answer: Thousands: those who participate in a feasibility study about the timeliness of a hymnal change; those who take part in a subsequent survey to rate the usefulness of all the items in the current hymnal or respond to an open call to submit new items for possible inclusion; those who write letters filled with suggestions to the project editor; those who apply and those who are appointed to the committee charged with making content decisions; those who field-test liturgical and other materials; those who attend music and worship conferences to learn about the possibilities of a new congregational song resource; those who attend General Assembly, learn what this new resource has to offer, and vote to endorse it for congregational use; those who participate in presbytery meetings where songs from a hymnal sampler are incorporated into workshops or worship services; those who serve on deliberative bodies in their local churches; those who make it possible for their congregations to purchase new hymnals without touching a penny of their operating budgets by donating books in memory or in honor of loved ones . . .

Unlike changing a light bulb, changing a hymnal requires a literal cast of thousands.

The list could go on and on. Unlike changing a light bulb, changing a hymnal requires a literal cast of thousands. Once every generation, groups undergo this labor-intensive process as a way of staying fresh in their worship and faithful to the God who does new things and calls for the singing of new songs.

"BESET BY CHANGE . . ."

But change is not easy—which is why the "Change?!?" answer to the light bulb joke evokes such a smile of recognition. Twenty-first-century congregations are no different from our forebears in this regard. Back in 1918, the great hymnal editor Louis Fitzgerald Benson noted with some chagrin:

> Even in our day of progress and enlarged resources a hymnbook in possession is not readily superseded by a revised edition. There are still Presbyterian congregations contented in the use of *The Presbyterian Hymnal* of 1874.[1]

So we might say, in *our* day of progress and enlarged resources (consider the sheer glut of material on the Internet), there are still congregations quite happy with the "blue" hymnal of 1990, the "old red" hymnal of 1955, and even the "green" one of 1933. Persuading such groups to let their current volumes be superseded by the "new red" or "purple" *Glory to God* of 2013 could be a tall order.

Sociologists who study the process of cultural innovation note that people fall into identifiable categories when it comes to accepting change.[2] A small number, around 2 percent, are *innovators*—people who come up with new ideas or develop new products. A further 18 percent are *early adopters*, enthusiasts who thrive on experimentation and enjoy their reputation as trendsetters. At the opposite end of the spectrum are 18 percent characterized as *late adopters,* who hold out against change, equally prizing their reputation as traditionalists; and another 2 percent of *never adopters,* those stalwart few for whom the "seven last words of the church" were coined: "We've never done it that way before." In between these extremes lies the vast majority of the population: the 60 percent of *middle adopters,* who take their time before making a decision but will eventually embrace a new idea if they can be persuaded that the benefits outweigh the risks.

Any church member can probably imagine faces to exemplify each of these categories: the cheerleaders, the critics, and the cautious questioners. Congregational leaders often end up in their positions because they possess the dispositions of innovators and early adopters. Indeed, ordination vows in the Presbyterian Church commit deacons, ruling elders, and teaching elders "to serve the people with energy, intelligence, *imagination*, and love" (W.4.4003[h]). The challenge for such visionary individuals is realizing that not everyone else immediately warms to new ideas . . . and that some people, in fact, will *never* warm to them, no matter how persuasive or compelling. Much energy can be lost in fixating on a few vocal opponents of innovation; much energy *should* be invested in addressing the concerns of those in the moderate middle.

Moderates resist innovation—whether a new hymnal, a new worship service, or a new format for the coffee hour—not so much from lack of vision as from fear of loss. As with the text of the Fred Pratt Green hymn used as the epigraph for this lesson, moderates feel *"beset* by change," assailed by perceived threats to something whose preservation they value. The songs chosen for worship serve as flash points for such fears because music is so significant in our lives of faith. Music touches us deeply, stirring up rich (and often pre-rational) associations with occasions when certain texts and tunes have been sung: a revival meeting attended with a beloved grandmother; a child's wedding; a parent's funeral. It is understandable, therefore, when churchgoers greet the proposal of a new hymnal with skepticism and reserve. Will the book contain the "old" hymns—whatever their actual date of composition—that are familiar and comfortable to *me*? Will I be able to sing the songs I know from memory without tripping over some textual alteration that a well-intentioned editorial committee has selected? Will someone else's theological or political or musical agenda rob me of those songs that bring a lift to my heart or a lump to my throat every time I sing them?

". . . BUT SPIRIT-LED"

Such questions are crucial for people deciding whether to adopt a new hymnal or figure out how to integrate a newly adopted one into worship. They are crucial as well for committees that revise hymnals from one generation to the next. Determining the ratio of familiar to new materials in any congregational song resource requires a balancing act: there must be enough "new" material to warrant the efforts that thousands will make to change the publication; but there must also be enough "old" material to reassure people that their traditions are being carried forward and that their "heart songs" will be preserved.

Within the Presbyterian family, different committees have handled this balance differently. The particular challenge for the group that created the 1990 *Presbyterian Hymnal: Hymns, Psalms, and Spiritual Songs* was that the customary twenty-year cycle of hymnal review and replacement had been altered by the publication of a joint hymn and liturgy resource, *The Worshipbook: Services and Hymns*, in 1975. Outstanding as this resource was, it did not gain widespread currency as a hymnal-proper—nor was it intended to do so. Half of its pages were dedicated to "orders for the public worship of God": services for baptism, confirmation, and receiving new members; for marriages and funerals; and for the Lord's Day, with or without the celebration of the Lord's Supper. This important focus on litanies and liturgies meant that the volume contained only about three hundred hymns, in contrast to the more than five hundred available in the *Hymnbook* of 1955.

As a result, congregations tended to keep the "red" *Hymnbook* in their pew racks to sing from. For the sake of familiarity and continuity, this was fortunate; for the sake of innovation, perhaps less so. By the time the "blue" 1990 hymnal appeared, a gap of *some thirty-five* years, rather than the customary *twenty*, separated the editions. Meanwhile, dramatic changes had been taking place in the world of church music. There was the "hymn explosion" of the 1960s; a growing interest in songs from formerly underrepresented parts of the globe; a new focus on social issues like ecology and inclusive language;

and experimentation with singing the Psalms differently from the traditional Presbyterian pattern of metric, rhyming verse. How was the committee to treat this abundance of material and at the same time produce a single book of reasonable size?

Although I did not sit on the 1990 hymnal committee, on the basis of my experience with the 2013 committee, I can imagine some of the excruciating choices the earlier group faced. To do justice to the rapidly changing hymnological scene, they weighted their collection toward newer material, with the result that only about 35 percent of hymns from the 1955 *Hymnbook* carried forward. This did not mean, however, that the remainder of the resulting 1990 collection was appearing for the first time ever in a Presbyterian hymnal. The intervening *Worshipbook* would have introduced congregations to songs like "Comfort, Comfort You My People" or "Earth and All Stars"—if congregations had used that intermediate collection.

In part because of the "Spirit-led" choices made by the 1990 committee, the task of the 2013 group, the PCOCS (or Presbyterian Committee on Congregational Song), was considerably easier. Research Services of the PC(USA) assisted the PCOCS by conducting a survey of congregations around the country to assess the frequency with which each item in the 1990 hymnal had been used, and the strength of support for carrying each forward. Our decisions in the PCOCS about content could thus be shaped by data telling us what songs from the 1990 hymnal had already become "heart songs." The PCOCS also benefited from correspondence—literally *hundreds* of e-mails and *thousands* of suggested pieces of music—telling us (among other things) which hymns from earlier hymnals people were acutely missing because they were not included in the 1990 book. This did not mean, however, that we made every selection on the basis of a popularity contest. In ways analogous to general Presbyterian polity, we recognized that the guidance of the Spirit can be made known through the voice of the wider congregation but that leaders are also expected to exercise personal judgment and not simply represent a majority view.

The end product of our prayerful deliberations is a collection that carries forward more than two-thirds of the hymns, psalms, and spiritual songs from the 1990 hymnal. It further includes a baker's dozen of "comeback" songs from the 1955 *Hymnbook* (e.g. "I Love to Tell the Story"), plus some "golden oldies" never before included in a Presbyterian hymnal intended for sanctuary worship (e.g. "Leaning on the Everlasting Arms" and other gospel songs more likely to have been used in Sunday school classes or Sunday evening services). Given advances in printing technology over the past two decades, *Glory to God* can contain more pages than the "blue" hymnal, in a book of the same size (and slightly lighter weight). This makes room for some 250 *more* pieces of music: 850-plus, in contrast to 605. The ultimate balance of "old" (defined as "appearing in the immediately prior hymnal") to "new" (not before in a Presbyterian denominational hymnal) is roughly half and half. The new hymnal will be even more familiar for congregations that have used the supplement *Sing the Faith*, as roughly a third of its 284 songs are carried forward.

"MUST CLAIM AND TEST ITS HERITAGE . . ."

But how exactly does a hymnal committee arrive at such decisions about what old material to carry forward and what new material to introduce? How does a single group "claim and test" the heritage of congregational song on behalf of the far wider church to whose service it is called? Having opened with a version of a light bulb joke, I am tempted to close with a variant of a different old chestnut: How do porcupines pass the peace?

The answer, of course, is "Very carefully." The process of the Presbyterian Committee on Congregational Song entailed four three-day meetings a year, beginning in August 2008 and ending in January 2012, with considerable work between gatherings. Courtesy of the Learning Asset Management Program, a program operated by a consortium of small, private liberal arts institutions in the southern Appalachians, we had a dedicated website enabling easy storage and retrieval of materials for discussion: our theological vision statement and language policy, correspondence from people outside the committee, meeting notes, study documents, and digital files of texts and tunes under consideration.

The PCOCS announced an "open submissions process" to invite suggestions from the wider church. We divided ourselves into three-person review teams consisting of a "music person," a "word person," and a third member who might have expertise in either area, to examine the *four thousand* items submitted. Week in and week out, each review team received ten to fifteen songs to assess. If two or more members of the team voted *yes*, the item moved forward for consideration by a subcommittee; if two-thirds of the subcommittee members said *yes*, the item moved to full committee review.

It is important to note that all information identifying the author, composer, and copyright holder was removed from each submitted item before evaluation occurred. Such anonymity remained in force from the beginning of the project until the end, when author and composer names were finally revealed to enable accurate editing. This scrupulosity about sources seemed particularly important since some authors and composers whose works were under consideration were also members of the committee, and we wanted to show no bias toward their works or those of any other contributor.

Beyond the subcommittee that received materials sent forward from review teams, we formed additional subgroups to focus on other bodies of work: a group with expertise in global song; one with experience in the use of "praise and worship" or contemporary Christian music; one to glean materials from the collections of contemporary composers and text writers who were recently deceased and thus not able to respond to an invitation to submit their work; one to sift through the contents of other hymnals published since the 1990 collection went to press. Hymns and songs that received favorable review from subcommittees came to the full committee to be read, sung, discussed, and voted on. Again, the full committee required a two-thirds majority vote for any text or tune to make its way onto the final contents list.

In total, the PCOCS "tested" some ten thousand items in order to claim roughly 850 as the heritage to be offered by the 2013 collection. Key questions guided this process. Does the text tell the faith story, transmit the biblical narrative, or serve a needed liturgical function; are the words poetically crafted and theologically sound? Is the music effective; could it be sung by a congregation lacking professional musical leadership as well as one rich in musical expertise? Does the piece progressively unfold its riches such that it will bear repeated singing and not grow trite after initial enthusiasm has faded? Does it offer a lasting gift to the church?

> . . . we were seeking contents for
> a body of worshipers with vastly differing needs,
> tastes, and traditions.

In considering such questions, we repeatedly reminded ourselves that we were not creating a collection of hymns that we as individuals happened to like; rather, we were seeking contents for a body of worshipers with vastly differing needs, tastes, and traditions. Like those porcupines passing the peace, we proceeded very carefully, recognizing that songs about which one group felt "prickly" might be the very songs to touch and transform their neighbors' hearts. Our work as a committee was thus influenced by attempts to consider the cast of thousands, both known and unknown, who would be affected by the process of hymnal change. We hope too that it was led by the Spirit, whose guidance we sought every step of the way.

NOTES

1. Louis Benson, "Shakespeare and the Metrical Psalms," *Journal of the Presbyterian Historical Society* 9, no. 6 (1918): 250.

2. Greg Scheer, *The Art of Worship: A Musician's Guide to Learning Modern Worship* (Grand Rapids: Baker Books, 2006), 24.

Chapter 3

THE THEOLOGY OF *GLORY TO GOD*

Carl Schalk, composer of the music for "God of the Sparrow" (#22) and numerous other hymns, once dryly remarked: "The problem with that song, 'I Love to Tell the Story' [#462], is that it doesn't tell the story!" He has a point. The lyrics by Katherine Hankey that were set to music by William Fischer in 1869 do not themselves detail the story of salvation. Instead, they describe the joys of sharing that story with others, whether those who "have never heard" or those who already "know it best."

To proclaim the salvation story in full would require significantly more than a single three-stanza hymn—but, to be fair, Hankey's original poem was over fifty stanzas long! Since modern-day congregations are unlikely to sing that many verses, we might propose instead that we need an entire *collection* of hymns to capture the magnitude of what God has done for us.

Glory to God is such a collection. The plotline of the 2013 hymnal follows the outline of salvation history, beginning with 380-some songs celebrating "God's Mighty Acts." The final 250 or so songs detail "Our Response to God." This dialogical framework reflects an insight expressed by twentieth-century Swiss theologian Karl Barth:

> Grace always demands the answer of gratitude.
> Grace and gratitude belong together like heaven and earth.
> Grace evokes gratitude like the voice of an echo.
> Gratitude follows grace like thunder follows lightning.[1]

Mediating these two sections, the center portion of the book focuses on the occasions where God's grace and our gratitude preeminently meet, in "The Church at Worship." Running as a steady theme through all these sections is "the old, old story of Jesus and his love."

THE TRIUNE GOD

The first subsection of "God's Mighty Acts," "The Triune God," fittingly includes texts exemplifying the most classical definition of a "hymn" as a song of praise or thanksgiving addressed *to* God. (Later definitions expand the category to include religious songs addressed to God's people, instructing them *about* God or about their responsibilities to one another and the rest of creation.) Most hymns in this section sing to God in the second person, using both traditional and contemporary pronouns: "Early in the morning, our song shall rise to *thee*" ("Holy, Holy, Holy! Lord God Almighty!" #1); "Holy God, We Praise *Your* Name" (#4). The mood of the music stretches from the awesome majesty of Isaiah's vision of holiness in the temple (Isaiah 6) to the shimmering delight of an early Christian image of *perichoresis*, according to which the three persons of the Trinity dance (*chore-*) around (*peri-*) one another in the perpetual interchanges of love ("The Play of the Godhead," #9).

Language used for the triune God is comparably diverse. In keeping with the "Statement on Language" crafted by the

Presbyterian Committee on Congregational Song (see chap. 8), hymns and songs draw from "the full reservoir of biblical imagery for God and God's gracious acts," employing both "metaphors that are comfortable in their familiarity and those that are enriching in their newness." "Come, Thou Almighty King" (#2) honors the Trinity with stanzas addressed to the "almighty King," the "incarnate Word," and the "holy Comforter." "Eternal Father, Strong to Save" (#8) sings to the "Father," "Savior," and "Holy Spirit." Doxologies appearing later in "The Church at Worship" sing to God as "Father, Son, and Holy Ghost" (#606) and as "Creator, Word, and Spirit" (#609) .

Such familiar names are complemented by other images. "Mothering God, You Gave Me Birth" (#7) picks up on allusions to God as a birth-giver (see, for example, Deut. 32:18). "Womb of Life and Source of Being" (#3) acknowledges the places where Old Testament references to God's "compassion" and "pity" play on Hebrew root words related to heart, womb, or inner parts (see Jer. 31:20 or Ps. 103). "Source and Sovereign, Rock and Cloud" (#11) catalogs multiple images for the three persons of the Trinity: among them, Fortress, Fountain, and Judge for the first stanza; Word, Wisdom, and Vine for the second; and Storm, Breath, and Dove for the third. "God the Sculptor of the Mountains" (#5) amplifies this list even further, identifying God with vivid biblical images such as "nuisance of the Pharaoh," "dresser of the vineyard," and "table-turning prophet." Children's sermons could elaborate for weeks on each of these images; youth could be challenged to scavenger hunts to find them all in the Bible. Christians of all ages could grow in our worship and prayer lives by expanding the ways in which we name the One who is above all names.

Christians of all ages could grow in our worship and prayer lives by expanding the ways in which we name the One who is above all names.

CREATION

The Christian theological plotline teaches that this triune God created the world in love and continues to guide and care for it. In texts that are familiar to us from *The Presbyterian Hymnal* (1990), God as Creator is honored as author of both the "sparrow" (#22) and the "spangled heavens" (#24). A hymn originally intended by its author/composer Natalie Sleeth for use with children sings to the "God of Great and God of Small" (#19) and honors the paradox that the Sovereign whom we worship is a "God of never-ending power, yet beside [us] every hour."

This paradox of transcendence and immanence captures an overarching perspective in *Glory to God*'s creation hymns. God is the powerful ruler over the forces of nature: "The Mighty God with Power Speaks" (#13) opens a version of Psalm 50, continuing with the line "and all the world obeys." The closing stanza of Isaac Watts's hymn "I Sing the Mighty Power of God" (#32) professes the faith that "clouds arise, and tempests blow, by order from thy throne." Yet, we might ask, are tempests like Hurricanes Sandy and Katrina also expressions of God's purposive will?

Such troubling questions require theological treatises for fuller discussion. But hymn writers and hymnal compilers have their own ways of responding. For *Glory to God,* this response takes the form of hymns in the "Creation and Providence" section that, like Natalie Sleeth's text, highlight God's intimate knowledge and protection of God's children, in and through the troubles we face. "Like a mother who has borne us" and "like a father who has taught us" (#44), God is our steady companion through life; God bears us up "on eagle's wings" (#43). Echoing the author of Lamentations 3:22, who wrote during his own time of national calamity, hymnist Thomas O. Chisholm encourages us to join in affirming: "Morning by morning, new mercies I see. . . . Great is thy faithfulness!" (#39).

As children of such a faithful Creator, we also have our responsibilities toward the creation. These are detailed more fully in the section of the hymnal dealing with "Our Response to God"—particularly in hymns focusing on "Dedication and Stewardship." "Touch the Earth Lightly" (#713) and "The Earth Belongs to God Alone" (#715) stand out as examples of texts calling us to care for the world God has made and commanded us to treat with respect.

COVENANT

But the God we worship is not just a God of nature. God also called a covenant people and entered into intimate relationship with them in history. In *Glory to God*, we sing of our forefather in "The God of Abraham Praise" (#49) and of our foremother in "To Abraham and Sarah the call of God was clear" (#51). We celebrate the exodus from Egypt in the traditional spiritual, "When Israel Was in Egypt's Land" (#52), with the familiar refrain "Go down, Moses." We also acknowledge the gift of the law in a metric setting of Psalm 119, "I Long for Your Commandments" (#64). Indeed, many of the Psalm settings in *Glory to God* can be found arranged topically in the section on God's covenant, giving voice to the ways our ancestors in the faith praised the God whom they knew to be active both in their individual and their national lives. Many settings of prophetic texts also appear in this section: "Surely, it is God who saves me" (#71) from Isaiah 12; and "Do not be afraid, for I am with you" (#76) from Isaiah 41; "You thirsty ones, come to the spring" (#78) and "You shall go out with joy" (#80), both from Isaiah 55.

CHRIST

God fulfilled the promises spoken through the prophets in the coming of the Christ child. Thus, hymns for the liturgical year, beginning with Advent, follow appropriately on the heels of hymns giving voice to covenant hope and continue throughout the sections of *Glory to God* dealing in turn with Christ's birth (Christmas), life (Lent), passion and death (Holy Week), resurrection (Easter), and ascension and reign. After the Hebrew people had waited long years for a Messiah, Mary conceived and bore a son and named him Jesus, a name rooted in the Hebrew verb meaning rescue or deliver, for "he will save his people from their sins" (Matt. 1:21). This work of salvation is too centrally important to confine to a few paragraphs, so it is discussed more fully in chapter 4.

THE HOLY SPIRIT

The story of salvation moves from Jesus' first coming in the incarnation to his second coming as judge and redeemer in the last days. In between those two climactic advents, we celebrate the sending of the Holy Spirit to give birth to the church. Two hymns in *Glory to God* sing about the momentous day in Jerusalem when the Spirit came with the rush of a mighty wind and descended on the apostles in tongues of flame: "On Pentecost They Gathered" (#289), which also appeared in the Presbyterian hymnbook of 1990, and "O Day of Joy and Wonder!" (#290), which is new to Presbyterian hymnals in 2013. In closing stanzas, both these Pentecost hymns ask for a fresh outpouring of the Spirit on believers in our day.

Numerous other songs from around the world also invoke the Spirit. Interestingly, the most frequent "first word" in the hymnal's first line index—after the multipurpose exclamation "O" (occurring sixty times)—is the verb "come," with thirty-four appearances. Many of these appearances are prayers for the Spirit's presence within and among us: "Come, Holy Ghost, Our Souls Inspire" (#278); "Come, Holy Spirit, Heavenly Dove"

(#279); "Come, O Spirit, Dwell Among Us" (#280); "Come, O Holy Spirit, Come" (#283). The last mentioned of these, also titled *Wa wa wa Emimimo*, hails from Nigeria by way of the musical transcription and English translation of a musical scholar from Taiwan. A further invocation of the Spirit, though with a different first word, has Tanzanian origins: "Gracious Spirit, Heed Our Pleading" (#287), with the refrain *Njoo, njoo, njoo, Roho mwema*.

Thirteen percent of the hymnal's contents originate from musical traditions whose songs were not available to the compilers of prior Presbyterian collections.

The last two hymns named above join many other songs from the global church to illustrate the truly pentecostal nature of *Glory to God*. Thirteen percent of the hymnal's contents originate from musical traditions whose songs were not available to the compilers of prior Presbyterian collections. In fact, music from six continents is represented in the book; texts and tunes from Asia, Africa, Australasia, and Latin America now complement the hymns and carols we have long loved to sing from the United States and Europe. This diverse body of music reminds us of a key teaching from the "Theological Vision Statement" of the Presbyterian Committee on Congregational Song (included here as chap. 5):

> The framework of the history of salvation offers a theological rationale for asking us to learn songs that come from cultures different from our own: Pentecost teaches us to speak and hear the gospel in many tongues and languages and only thus, "with all the saints," to comprehend the breadth and length and height and depth of the love of Christ (Eph. 3:18). We do not sing hymns and songs because they were birthed in our

culture; we sing them because they teach us something about the richness that is in God.

THE CHURCH

The frequency with which the word "come" is used as a first word in hymns illustrates more than a heartfelt longing for the presence and power of the Holy Spirit. It also speaks to a hunger in our day for community, for the body of believers called into being on that first Pentecost to "come together" as a family of welcome. "Come All You People" (#388, *Uyai mose*) from Zimbabwe invites all to "come and praise [our] Maker." "Come, Ye Sinners, Poor and Needy" (#415) from the U.S. folk tradition joins forces with "Come, Ye Thankful People, Come" (#367) from the ranks of beloved Victorian hymns and "Come to the Table" (#508) from the contemporary Korean American Presbyterian community. "Come Sing, O Church, in Joy!" (#305)—the hymn that won the competition for a text celebrating the bicentennial of the Presbyterian church in this country in 1988–1989—calls us to celebrate our ongoing journey "in bold accord."

Such accord is surely needed. Some analysts have said that our current cultural climate in the United States is as polarized as during the Civil War. When caught in such tensions, we can be helped—and perhaps, to a degree, healed—by singing together: "We Are One in the Spirit" (#300) or "We Are One in Christ Jesus" (#322, *Somos uno en Cristo*). Singing elevates our endorphin levels, sending small surges of natural body opiates through our bloodstream. This is why listening to music gives us chills, and singing together can make us feel for a moment as if all is right with the world—that we might truly live, metaphorically as well as literally, *in harmony* with one another. Singing of God's welcome becomes in itself an act of welcome. Brought together into one body, shored up by "The

Church's One Foundation" (#321), which is Jesus Christ, our Lord, we are also strengthened for mission and discipleship. "Lord, You Give the Great Commission" (#298), we sing; or putting Jesus' command onto our own lips, we exhort one another, "Go to the World!" (#295).

THE LIFE OF THE NATIONS

When we go to the world, we discover that God is still present with us, as with our forebears in the covenant, working to bring about the long-awaited reign of justice and peace. As in the hymnals of 1933 and 1955, so in *Glory to God,* "patriotic" hymns occur within this broader context of the anticipated "kingdom of God on earth": hymns like "My Country 'Tis of Thee" (#337), "O Beautiful for Spacious Skies" (#338), and "Lift Every Voice and Sing" (#339). When we sing our way through this chapter of the story of God's mighty acts, we find prayers for our homeland complemented by prayers *for* all nations—"This Is My Song" (#340) and "For the Healing of the Nations" (#346). We find, as well, prayers *from* all nations—"From All That Dwell Below the Skies" (#327), with a text from Great Britain and a tune from Germany, and "Praise God, All You Nations" (#328), with a text from the Psalms and a tune from Ghana.

A NEW HEAVEN AND A NEW EARTH

As we sing of our national life, we not only profess our praise to God but also confess that we live "In an Age of Twisted Values" (#345). So we yearn for that coming day when the "Judge Eternal, Throned in Splendor" (#342) will "cleanse the body of this nation through the glory of the Lord." Hymns further anticipating Christ's return and judgment are discussed in chapter 4.

But that judgment is ultimately transformed into joy, because it heralds God's new creation. As in hymns found earlier in the chapter on God's covenant with ancient Israel, here again images from the prophets stir our hearts. "O day of peace that dimly shines" (#373); "Dream On, Dream On" (#383) from Korea; and "We Wait the Peaceful Kingdom" (#378) all develop the incomparable poetry of Isaiah: the wolf will dwell with the lamb, spears will be hammered into pruning hooks, and a little child will lead the way. *Glory to God* balances hymns that celebrate a this-worldly realization of *shalom* with those who anticipate a heavenly realm—a realm where we "gather at the river; where bright angel feet have trod" (#375), and "We Fall Down" (#368) and "lay our crowns at the feet of Jesus."

Here, we enter into a realm beyond our wildest imaginings, a world where words ultimately fail and all we have left is song: "And we cry, holy, holy, holy." It is the best possible ending to the greatest story ever told. Glory be to God!

NOTE

1. Karl Barth, *Church Dogmatics,* IV/1, 41.

Chapter 4

TEACHINGS ON SALVATION IN *GLORY TO GOD*

"Hear the good news of salvation!" These words (*Wotanin waste nahon po* in their original language) open a hymn written by the first Native American Dakota ordained as a Presbyterian minister (#441). They might well be inscribed above the entrance to every sanctuary and on the flyleaf of every hymnal. Without the gospel of Jesus Christ—who was born; who suffered; who was crucified, died, and was buried; and who rose again—we would have no churches at all, and certainly no collections of Christian songs to sing within them. So, it is centrally important to ask of any hymnal what it has to say about this good news. Below are eight teachings on salvation illustrated by hymns, psalms, and spiritual songs from *Glory to God*.

1. Human beings are sinners who regularly need to confess our sin.

Not every group in the Christian family places as strong an emphasis on confession as Presbyterians do. In some denominations, a prayer of confession figures only occasionally—for example, in a communion liturgy to help people prepare to receive the sacrament. But according to the pattern of Reformed worship (found in the liturgical materials in *Glory to God*), a time for "Confession and Pardon" appears in *each* Service for the Lord's Day at the close of the time of "Gathering," immediately prior to the proclamation of the Word. The Reformed tradition teaches that before we can receive what God has to offer us in Scripture, we need to cleanse our hearts and our hearing.

> The Reformed tradition teaches that before we can receive what God has to offer us in Scripture, we need to cleanse our hearts and our hearing.

Consequently, the section of *Glory to God* devoted to "The Church at Worship" contains twenty hymns specifically labeled "Confession." In fact, the very middle hymns of the whole hymnal—numbers 426 and 427 out of the total of 853—fall within the Confession category: a haunting Taiwanese refrain echoing Psalm 139, "Search Me, O God"; and a Pashto hymn from the regions of Afghanistan and Pakistan, "Jesus Knows the Inmost Heart," whose first stanza admits: "This our sinful hearts require: flame of God's refining fire." The need for confession of sin is, therefore, quite literally a *central* teaching of *Glory to God*.

In addition to songs from the global church, other genres also offer confession in song. *Glory to God* includes three different settings of Psalm 51, the text traditionally attributed to King David, written after his sins in seducing Bathsheba and arranging for her husband's death in battle. Two of these—"Create in Me a Clean Heart" (#422) and "Create in Me a Clean Heart, O God" (#423)—have a contemporary musical flavor. The third, "Have Mercy, God, upon My Life" (#421), is a twenty-first-century text set to an eighteenth-century tune, falling squarely within the tradition of metrical Psalms out of the Genevan and Scottish Reformations.

But confession, according to Reformed theology, is not simply for individual sins. While we may well sing in the first-person singular, "Create in *me* a clean heart," we also acknowledge that sin exists in the first-person plural, at the bitter root of *our* failure to create communities of justice, peace, and love. "Forgive Us, Lord (*Perdón, Señor*)" (#431) appears in *Glory to God* in both English and Spanish and begs forgiveness for an array of sins that we commit both as individuals and as societies: "grievance and injustice," "aloofness and indifference." Further texts confessing our failures to follow God's will, tend our human neighbors, and care for our natural environment appear throughout the section of the hymnal titled "Justice and Reconciliation."

2. Like our ancestors in the faith, we have fallen out of right relationship and "deserve God's condemnation," to use words from the PC(USA) Brief Statement of Faith that appears in the front section of Glory to God.

Glory to God does not ignore the judgment we merit. "Judge Eternal, Throned in Splendor" (#342, a hymn from the 1955 *Hymnbook* that makes a comeback in 2013) uses imagery like that of the Pashto hymn referenced above (or like Malachi 3:2), praying: "with your living fire of judgment / purge this land of bitter things." A metric version of Psalm 2, "Why Do Nations Rage Together" (#758), acknowledges that "God's wrath is quickly kindled" against those who do not "serve the Lord." The sin of our forebears who forsook the covenant is brought into the present with "In an Age of Twisted Values" (#345), a hymn confessing our "struggle for possessions," our "prejudice and fear," our conflict-riddled communities and families—and, we might add, our divisive and divided churches. "All Who Love and Serve Your City" (#351) powerfully announces that "all days are days of judgment" and prays that God come quickly as "our judge, our glory" to a waiting and a wanting world.

3. Because our forebears violated God's covenant, God gave the gift of the law and sent prophets repeatedly to call them—and us—back to obedience.

Glory to God follows the narrative of salvation history in its presentation of hymns, particularly in the first major section, which focuses on "God's Mighty Acts." This outline allows a full section for sustained consideration of God's covenant with our forebearers in the faith. "Deep in the Shadows of the Past" (#50) sings of our nomadic ancestors who "by their tents, around their fires in story, song, and law" recorded God's revealed promises. "I Long for Your Commandments" (#64), a portion of Psalm 119, voices our need for God's wisdom, without which we "stumble in the dark." The law, thus understood, does not restrain our freedom in burdensome ways; rather, as John Calvin points out in his "third use" of the law, it rescues us from chaos, training us and enabling us to flourish as individuals and communities. A metric version of Psalm 19 further exclaims, "Your Law, O Lord, Is Perfect" (#61), celebrating the life and health to be found in teachings whose taste is "like sweet honey."

Glory to God follows the narrative of salvation history in its presentation of hymns, particularly in the first major section, which focuses on "God's Mighty Acts."

Yet, despite this sweetness, we spurn God's law, for which reason prophets have been sent to call us back to paths of right living. The teaching of Micah 6:8 finds its way, almost word for word, into a popular, three-part round newly included in *Glory to God*, "What Does the Lord Require of You?" (#70): "to seek justice and love kindness and walk humbly with your God." Even with such teachings to guide us, though, we persist in sin. The second stanza of a hymn detailing what "Isaiah the Prophet Has Written of Old" (#77) provides a sad commentary on our disobedience: "nations still prey on the meek of the world, and conflict turns parent from child. [God's] people despoil all the sweetness of earth. . . ." Or, as we affirm in our Brief Statement of Faith:

> Ignoring God's commandments,
> we violate the image of God in others and ourselves,
> . . . .
> exploit neighbor and nature,
> and threaten death to the planet entrusted to our care.

4. *Continuing to seek us out, God sent Jesus into the world to be the Messiah, the long-awaited Savior.*

Advent and Christmas texts in abundance illustrate this point. Numerous beloved carols and hymns extol the mystery of God's birth among us, prompting us to rejoice: "Love has come, a light in the darkness!" (#110); "Joy to the world, the Lord is come!" (#134). Wonder and thanksgiving for the matchless gift of Emmanuel are the predominant motifs in hymns illustrating this fourth theological point.

In addition to such notes of celebration, however, a few texts in *Glory to God* also anticipate the costliness of the incarnation. Versions of the Annunciation and the Magnificat warn of the price to be paid by the powerful of earth. In "No Wind at the Window" (#101), the visiting angel cautions: "'This child must be born that the kingdom might come: salvation for many, destruction for some.'" In "My Soul Cries Out with a Joyful Shout" (#100), Mary warns that tyrants will be cast from their thrones, and "the spear and rod [will] be crushed by God." Boldly, she cries out to the Holy One: "Let the fires of your justice burn."

But in the process of establishing justice, this Holy One will also pay a price. In its section of hymns on the birth of Jesus, *Glory to God* contains the version of William Chatterton Dix's "What Child Is This" (#145) first published in the *Oxford Book of Carols*, in which the stanza, "Why lies he in such mean estate" goes on to proclaim: "Nails, spear shall pierce him through, the cross be borne for me, for you." Richard Wilbur's captivating hymn in the section on Jesus' life, "A Stable Lamp Is Lighted" (#160), moves in the space of three stanzas from stars that herald a miraculous birth to a sky that will "groan and darken" as Jesus is "forsaken and yielded up to die." Given the number of people for whom the relentless cultural pressure for cheeriness around the holidays causes deep pain (because, for example, they are dealing with personal losses or grieving over circumstances in the world), a hymnal can offer helpful reminders of God's presence with us as one who has also known grief, who comes bringing light to those who sit in darkness and in the shadow of death.

5. Jesus preached, taught, and healed, commanding us to follow him into lives of mission and service.

Just as the salvation history framework of *Glory to God* opens new space for songs devoted to God's covenant with Jesus' ancestors and our own, so it also makes room for more texts about Jesus' life—the words he spoke and the wonders he performed between the climactic moments of his birth and his death and resurrection. He called disciples: "Will you leave yourself behind if I but call your name?" ("Will You Come and Follow Me," #726). He pronounced blessing on those who "show mercy," "seek peace," and "suffer hate" for his sake ("Blest Are They," #172). He ministered to outcasts ("The Woman Hiding in the Crowd," #178; "Ten Lepers

Facing Constant Scorn," #179). He challenged the powerful elite of his day, "danc[ing] for the scribe and the Pharisee," who refused to countenance his unconventional ministry ("I Danced in the Morning," #157). He charged disciples to carry forth his work in the world ("Go to the World!" #295; "Lord, You Give the Great Commission," #298).

In turn, *we* are "Called as Partners in Christ's Service" (#761), in the words of a much-loved text carried forward from the 1990 hymnal: "Christ's example, Christ's inspiring, Christ's clear call to work and worth, let *us* follow, never faltering." In a song from the recent Roman Catholic liturgical renewal, we are bid to "Come! Live in the Light!" (#749). A rousing gospel arrangement following the African American practice of adapting earlier hymn texts (in this instance, Charles Wesley's "Hark! The Herald Angel Sing," #119) proclaims Jesus to be the Light of the World, responding: "We'll walk in the light" ("Hark! The Herald Angels Sing," #127). In a hymn by a Cuban Pentecostal pastor—"The Lord Now Sends Us Forth (*Enviado soy de Dios*)" (#747)—*we* affirm in both English and Spanish:

The Lord now sends us forth	*Eviado soy de Dios,*
with hands to serve and give,	*mi mano lista está*
to make of all the earth	*para construir con él*
a better place to live.	*un mundo fraternal.*

6. This same Jesus died on the cross for our sake, put to death by sinful human beings.

Countless classic hymns of the faith embed this teaching deeply in our hearts. The spiritual "Were You There" (#228) carries the implication that each of us in some way *was* at the cross, complicit in the suffering of innocence through our sins of commission or omission. The chorale, "O Sacred Head, Now Wounded" (#221) admits: "mine, mine was the transgression, but thine, the deadly pain." "Rock of Ages, Cleft for Me" (#438), restored from the 1955 *Hymnbook*, implores: "Let the water and the blood from thy wounded side which flowed be of sin the double cure." (Interestingly: Baptist and Methodist hymnals have traditionally ended that stanza: "Save from wrath and make me pure." Presbyterian hymnals since 1874 have opted instead for the line: "Save me from its guilt and power.")

Newer hymns, as well, carry forward this theology. From the contemporary praise and worship canon in the United States, Twila Paris's "Your Only Son: Lamb of God" (#518) confesses, "Your gift of love we crucified; we laughed and scorned him as he died." From the praise and worship tradition out of Korea, we sing of Jesus who "with his blood has washed and healed me, paid the heavy cost" ("To My Precious Lord," #704). A twenty-first-century neoclassical hymn text, "Rejected and Despised" (#222), provides a sung version of the Suffering Servant passages from Isaiah 52–53, further locating God's compassionate presence alongside "all the victims of our age" and concluding: "In scourge-marked flesh we find our Christ, and by his stripes are healed."

7. God raised Jesus from the dead, conquering death itself, breaking the hold of evil over our lives and our world.

Throughout its history, Christian theology has held many views of how God accomplished our salvation in Jesus. The great ecumenical councils never came to a single position on atonement as they did for the Trinity or for Christology. As the PC(USA) Confession of 1967 teaches, "God's reconciling act in Jesus Christ is a mystery which the Scriptures describe in various ways. . . . [as] expressions of a truth which remains beyond the reach of all theory" (*Book of Confessions,* 9.09). So, in addition to the imagery of Jesus' dying for our sake (taking our punishment, paying our debt), another theological perspective—sometimes referred to as *Christus Victor*—speaks of the cross and resurrection as a conquest of evil powers. The exemplary hymn of this genre is "A Mighty Fortress Is Our God" (#275), which exults in the fact that we need no longer tremble at "the Prince of Darkness grim": "his doom is sure," as Christ "must win the battle."

Newer hymns and songs also reflect the *Christus Victor* motif. John Bell of the Iona Community has put to music a text from Archbishop Desmond Tutu that proclaims "Goodness Is Stronger than Evil" (#750) and voices the bracing affirmation: "Victory is ours, through God who loves us!" An Easter hymn from Tanzania, "Christ Has Arisen, Alleluia" (#251) focuses more on the victory over death than that over evil, with the exultant refrain:

> Let us sing praise to him with endless joy.
> Death's fearful sting he has come to destroy.

The "Service Music" section of *Glory to God* contains two contemporary settings of the "Memorial Acclamation" sometimes used in the celebration of the Lord's Supper: "Dying you destroyed our death; rising you restored our life" (#567, #570). All such musical offerings enable us to sing what we believe in Christ's death and resurrection: God has triumphantly ushered in the new creation that will come to full flowering when Christ returns in glory.

8. Jesus will come again, bringing a day of judgment that is also a day of joy.

The "God's Mighty Acts" section of *Glory to God* closes with subsections labeled "Christ's Return and Judgment" and "A New Heaven and a New Earth." Hymns in these sections command us to stand "in fear and trembling" as Christ our God descends to earth, demanding our full homage ("Let All Mortal Flesh Keep Silence," #347). They warn us that God "is trampling out the vintage where the grapes of wrath are stored" ("Mine Eyes Have Seen the Glory," #354, alluding to Isaiah 63). In the words of a popular praise chorus, "Our God Is an Awesome God" (#616), whose reign combines wisdom, power, and love. This power is not to be trifled with.

Yet, the love of God is what prevails. The bridegroom flings open the doors, inviting us to a wedding feast ("'Sleepers, Wake!' A Voice Astounds Us," #349). "We Fall Down" (#368) before "the greatness of mercy and love at the feet of Jesus." "Love Divine, All Loves Excelling" (#366) completes the new creation, making us "pure and spotless" at last. A text by nineteenth-century Scottish minister John Ross Macduff, "Christ Is Coming!" (#360), fittingly gives the final word to hope:

> Christ is coming! Let creation
> from its groans and labor cease;
> let the glorious proclamation
> hope restore and faith increase:
> Christ is coming! Christ is coming!
> Come, O blessed Prince of peace.
>
> Earth can now but tell the story
> of your bitter cross and pain;
> we shall yet behold your glory,
> Lord, when you return to reign:
> Christ is coming! Christ is coming!
> Let each heart repeat the strain.

Let the church say: Amen!

Chapter 5

THEOLOGICAL VISION STATEMENT

Collections of hymns, psalms, and spiritual songs give voice to the church's core beliefs and theological convictions. Their texts are "compact theology,"[1] and the selection of hymns and songs, the order in which they are presented, and even the ways in which they are indexed shape the theological thinking and ultimately the faith and practices of the church.

Previous hymnals have responded to the needs of the church and the world by highlighting the rhythms of the church year, the centrality of the psalms in the prayer and praise of Reformed churches, the corporate witness of the church to the world, the seeking of God's peace and God's justice, and the rich musical and poetic resources of world Christianity. All these motifs remain important and should be retained, in one way or another, in this collection.

This collection of hymns and songs, however, will be published amid different conditions than those that molded previous hymnals. It will be offered in a world in which trust in human progress has been undermined and where eclectic spiritualities often fail to satisfy deep spiritual hungers. It will be used by worshipers who have not had life-long formation by Scripture and basic Christian doctrine, much less Reformed theology. It is meant for a church marked by growing diversity in liturgical practice. Moreover, it addresses a church divided by conflicts but nonetheless, we believe, longing for healing and the peace that is beyond understanding.

To inspire and embolden a church facing these formidable challenges, the overarching theme of this collection will be God's powerful acts of creation, redemption, and final transformation. It will also bespeak the human responses that God's gracious acts make possible. In other words, the framework for this collection of congregational song will be the history of salvation.

> To inspire and embolden a church facing formidable challenges, the overarching theme of this collection will be God's powerful acts of creation, redemption, and final transformation.

This theme of salvation history answers the needs of the church and the world in the following ways:

- The priority placed on God's acts offers hope to those whose faith in human efforts has been undermined.
- A focus on salvation history reminds a church and world riddled with anxiety, frustration, and conflict that love has come to earth and that the risen and ascended Christ is alive and active.
- The emphasis on God's provision for us invites our grateful response. It makes a place for expressions of corporate commitment as well as personal devotion.
- The framework of salvation history is widely inclusive. It has places for existing hymns and invites the writing of new words and music to supply major omissions.

It makes room for the whole of the biblical witness, not only psalms and the Gospels that are already well reflected in hymn texts, but also the segments of the Scriptures that are not. It incorporates the events of the Christian year, the sacraments, and the mission of the church throughout the world as Christ's living body.
- As such, this framework both encompasses and enriches the liturgical practices that exist in the church. It includes the christological rhythm of the liturgical year, from Advent to the Reign of Christ, but also places the liturgical year in the wider framework of God's covenantal acts in creation and toward Israel. It challenges all users, whatever liturgical patterns they use, to shape their worship by the full extent of the biblical narrative.
- The rich narrative of salvation history—with the life stories of people like Abraham and Sarah, Eli and Samuel, Boaz and Ruth, Philip and the Ethiopian eunuch—makes audible the manifold ways in which God engages people of different ages, nationalities, races, and genders.

> We do not sing hymns and songs because they were birthed in our culture; we sing them because they teach us something about the richness that is in God.

- The framework of the history of salvation offers a theological rationale for asking us to learn songs that come from cultures different from our own: Pentecost teaches us to speak and hear the gospel in many tongues and languages and only thus, "with all the saints," to comprehend the breadth and length and height and depth of the love of Christ (Eph. 3:18). We do not sing hymns and songs because they were birthed in our culture; we sing them because they teach us something about the richness that is in God.

- Likewise, the notion of salvation history invites us to bridge the divide between different musical styles and traditions. As scribes who have been trained for God's reign will bring out of their treasures "what is new and what is old" (Matt. 13:52), so musicians are invited to lead us in songs both old and new, in praise of a God who is the first and the last, the ancient of everlasting days, and the Lord of the new creation.

—Ratified by the Presbyterian Committee on Congregational Song (PCOCS), February 2009

NOTE

1. "Compact theology" is a phrase used by the late David Allan Hubbard, biblical scholar and president of Fuller Seminary, to describe hymn texts.

Chapter 6

LITURGY IN *GLORY TO GOD*

"Glory to God in the highest heaven" (Luke 2:14). The Christian story begins with worship—the heavenly hymn of the heavenly host, singing praise at the birth of Jesus in Bethlehem. *Glory to God*, the 2013 Presbyterian hymnal, also begins with worship—almost fifty pages of liturgical texts:

- The Service for the Lord's Day, including the Lord's Supper
- The Sacrament of Baptism and the Reaffirmation of the Baptismal Covenant
- Services for Daily Prayer
  - Morning Prayer
  - Midday Prayer
  - Evening Prayer
  - Prayer at the Close of Day
- Other Texts for Worship (in English, Spanish, and Korean)

- Nicene Creed
- Apostles' Creed
- Lord's Prayer
- The Law of God
- Summary of the Law
- A Brief Statement of Faith

This chapter will help you make good use of these worship resources as your congregation welcomes the arrival of the new Presbyterian hymnal, *Glory to God*.

OLD, NEW, BORROWED, BLUE

The worship resources in *Glory to God* are simultaneously traditional, contemporary, ecumenical, and Reformed—or to put it another way: "old, new, borrowed, and blue." They are *old*—ancient, in fact—rooted in the earliest patterns and practices of the Christian tradition: gathering around Word and sacrament to celebrate Jesus' resurrection on the first day of the week; welcoming new members of Christ's body through washing with water and the anointing of the Spirit; keeping daily disciplines of study, self-offering, devotion, and prayer. They are *new*—reflecting contemporary changes in Christian worship, fresh approaches to liturgy and language, and recent initiatives toward sacramental renewal. These worship resources are *borrowed*—in the sense that they draw on a wealth of wisdom from the larger church and demonstrate our deep commitment to ecumenical dialogue. And they are "true *blue*"—faithful to the principles at the heart of the Reformed/Presbyterian tradition: the centrality of Scripture in Christian faith, life, and liturgy; the presence of Christ in Word and sacrament as "notes of the church"; a dynamic relationship between form and freedom through the ordering of the Word and the gifts of the Spirit; and the value of worship in the vernacular or common language of the people of God.

The liturgical texts in *Glory to God* are largely drawn from the 1993 Presbyterian *Book of Common Worship* (*BCW*) and are designed in accordance with the Directory for Worship (DFW) of the Presbyterian Church (U.S.A.). However, as indicated above, they also take into account two decades of further development in the church and culture. The intent of these liturgies is not to dictate a set order of service but to provide one exemplary, accessible model for Reformed worship in the twenty-first century. Careful readers will see that the rubrics (red print) in each section provide multiple options, encourage creativity, invite spontaneity, and rely on the leading of the Spirit in all things. The word "may"—emblematic of the freedom and flexibility in these rubrics—is found nearly one hundred times in fifty pages!

The intent of these liturgies is not to dictate a set order of service but to provide one exemplary, accessible model for Reformed worship in the twenty-first century.

THE SERVICE FOR THE LORD'S DAY

The Service for the Lord's Day provided in *Glory to God* follows the Presbyterian *Book of Common Worship* in presenting a fourfold pattern for Sunday worship: gathering, Word, Eucharist, and sending. Those who are familiar with the fivefold order of worship in the 1989 PC(USA) Directory for Worship may wonder: What about "Responding to the Word?" The Service for the Lord's Day in *Glory to God* reflects the conviction that *everything* in Christian faith, life, and worship is a response to God's gracious initiative in Jesus Christ, the Word made flesh. Accordingly, *everything* that happens in Sunday worship—from beginning to end—is a response to the Word who gathers, teaches, nourishes, and sends us. The Affirmation of

Faith and Prayers of the People (found under "Responding" in the DFW) are placed in the Word section of the liturgy in *Glory to God* (as in the *BCW*); similarly, the element of offering (found under "Responding" in the DFW) becomes the first part of the liturgy for the Eucharist or Lord's Supper (as in the *BCW*).

Furthermore, the Service for the Lord's Day in *Glory to God* assumes that Word and Eucharist are integrally related—that is, that the proclamation of the Word and the celebration of the sacraments belong together in the church's worship on the Lord's Day. This is a deeply Reformed conviction, one that can be traced to John Calvin's understanding of the church and desire for its worship. It is a pattern of worship that comes to us from the earliest Christian communities, as the second-century testimony of Justin Martyr demonstrates. Most importantly, it is rooted in the biblical account of Jesus' own interpretation of Scripture and breaking of bread on the day he rose from the dead (Luke 24).

Gathering

Through this first movement in the Service for the Lord's Day we enact our identity—as the people of God, redeemed by Jesus Christ, united in the Spirit as members of Christ's body. All the elements in the liturgy for gathering serve this end: we hear sentences of Scripture as the voice of the Word of God who calls us to worship; we greet one another in Jesus' name; we sing praise to the glory of God, the giver of our life; we call on the power of God's Word and Spirit as we meet for worship; we confess our unworthiness to enter God's presence but give thanks for the grace of Jesus Christ, in whose name we are forgiven.

The rubrics suggest leading the confession and pardon from the baptismal font, pouring water as the Call to Confession is spoken and lifting water at the Declaration of Forgiveness. These actions—new to the Service for the Lord's Day in *Glory to God*—reflect a decade of work toward sacramental renewal in the PC(USA) and a deeper emphasis on the meaning and mystery of our baptism. The intent is to offer a regular opportunity to remember one's baptism—a sign of the gift of Christ's grace and the calling to walk in newness of life to the glory of God.

The music ("Lord, Have Mercy," "Glory to God") provided here and elsewhere in the Service for the Lord's Day is from a setting by the popular and prolific Presbyterian composer Hal Hopson. By having music embedded in the liturgy, these resources remind worship planners of the power of music to engage the congregation as full participants in prayer and praise. This setting was chosen for its simplicity, strength, and "singability"; many other service music settings are provided in "The Church at Worship" section of *Glory to God*.

Word

In the service of the Word we not only hear the ancient words of Scripture but listen for the voice of Jesus Christ—the living Word—who continues to speak to the church, to the world, and in our daily lives. Because we rely on the power of the Holy Spirit to reveal Christ through the Word read and proclaimed, we begin with a Prayer for Illumination. The eucharistic prayer (or Great Thanksgiving) and Thanksgiving Over the Water in baptism contain similar prayers for the presence of Christ in the power of the Spirit. Next there are readings from Scripture—ordinarily from the Old and New Testaments as a witness to the full measure of God's revelation. The liturgy in *Glory to God* offers guidelines on how the readings of the Revised Common Lectionary might be used most effectively in worship; scriptural and lectionary indexes in the back of the hymnal will help worship planners to match hymns with these and other Scriptures. As in the *BCW*, there is the option of special responses to frame the reading of the Gospel; these words do not seek to elevate one reading over others but to lift up the Lord Jesus Christ, the Word to whom the Scriptures bear witness. Through the sermon that follows, the teaching elder (or pastor) seeks to open God's Word to the congregation, inviting them to open their lives to God and be transformed.

After the Scriptures and sermon, other actions flow from the reading and proclamation of the Word: an Invitation to Discipleship, a song of commitment or praise, an Affirmation of Faith, the Sacrament of Baptism (see below) or another pastoral rite of the church, the Prayers of the People, and the sharing of Christ's peace, if not included earlier in the service. The rubrics note that it is especially appropriate for a ruling elder or deacon to lead the Prayers of the People, either from the Lord's Table or from the midst of the congregation. This suggestion seeks to encourage greater engagement on the part of other ordered ministries (besides pastors) in the nurture of the congregation, the discipline of prayer, the ministry of pastoral care, and the mission of the church in the world.

Eucharist

Eucharist means "thanksgiving." It comes from the Greek verb *eucharisteo* that frequently appears when Jesus breaks bread with his disciples—both with the loaves and fish beside the sea and at the Passover meal before his death. Paul uses the same word when he recounts the institution of the Lord's Supper in his first letter to the church at Corinth. The word "Eucharist" helps to convey the essential nature of this sacramental meal as a joyful feast of gratitude for God's grace in Jesus Christ. It may be used alongside other terms for the sacrament: Lord's

Supper, emphasizing the institution of the meal by the Lord Jesus Christ, and Communion, suggesting the common bond of the Spirit that unites those who share this feast.

The structure of the eucharistic liturgy is shaped by the Gospel stories of Jesus' meals—in the feeding of the multitude, on the eve of his death, and on the day of his resurrection. Each of these accounts reveals another fourfold pattern in the action of Jesus: taking, blessing, breaking, and giving. The church has "translated" these Greek verbs into elements of the eucharistic liturgy: offering gifts, giving thanks, breaking bread, and distributing it among the people.

The eucharistic liturgy in *Glory to God* thus begins with offering—not only the presentation of financial gifts but the preparation of the table and the collection of food for the hungry, as a rubric indicates. Ruling elders or deacons may lead the prayer of dedication, reflecting their respective roles as stewards of the community's gifts and leaders in the church's service to the poor. The invitation to the table provided in *Glory to God* frames the movement from Word and Eucharist with a reference to the Emmaus story of Luke 24 (cited above).

> Ruling elders or deacons may lead the prayer of dedication, reflecting their respective roles as stewards of the community's gifts and leaders in the church's service to the poor.

With a few exceptions, the great thanksgiving in *Glory to God* is "all rubrics"—encouraging presiders to learn the ancient form of the liturgy while inviting seasonal variation, creative development, and extemporaneous prayer. The exceptions are worth noting. First, the words of institution are provided in the midst of the eucharistic prayer (one of three options in the DFW). This placement keeps the narrative of Jesus' meal "on the night before he died" at the *center* of the rite; at the same time, it allows for other words from Scripture (see below) at the breaking of the bread, setting the stage for a joyful feast with the *risen* Lord. Second, the prayer for the Holy Spirit is "spelled out," both because of its significance in Reformed sacramental theology (highlighting the role of the Spirit in the efficacy of the Sacrament) and because of its importance in ecumenical dialogue. Third, a Trinitarian doxology concludes the prayer, recapitulating the Trinitarian structure of the whole Great Thanksgiving. As noted above, embedded musical responses point to the role of music in enhancing congregational participation in the prayer.

After the Great Thanksgiving, the contemporary, ecumenical version of the Lord's Prayer is provided. This choice reflects the Reformed value of worship in the common language of the people (versus a form of English that hasn't been spoken for several hundred years). The breaking of the bread follows, with suggested words from John 6:35 and 15:5; evocative and easily memorized, these sentences of Scripture will help set the tone for a resurrection meal. Suggestions of congregational songs from *Glory to God* are offered for singing during the Communion of the People—another effective way to enhance the celebration of the sacrament. Following the Prayer after Communion, words are provided to accompany the extended service of communion, in which deacons or ruling elders take the message of the gospel, the bread, and the cup to homebound or hospitalized members immediately after worship. This is another new development in *Glory to God*, encouraging other ordered ministers to exercise their spiritual gifts in pastoral care.

Sending

In the rite of sending, the church is commissioned for participation in God's mission. The service of God in public worship prepares the way for the service of God in public life. The Greek noun *leitourgia* (meaning "work of the people"), from which we get the word "liturgy," conveys this double sense of public worship and public work or witness. The Hebrew verb *'avad*, used repeatedly in Exodus, also captures this dual meaning: "'Let my people go, so that they may worship me'" (Exod. 9:1).

A rubric at the beginning of the sending indicates that this is a good place for "brief announcements related to the church's mission." Placing such announcements here will help to show how the church's service in the world flows from the service of worship. The hymn, psalm, or song that follows should convey the church's commitment to Christ's mission, as a grateful response to God's grace. Notice that the blessing precedes the charge in this order of worship (another new development in *Glory to God*). This order is a "missional" move; it reflects the understanding that we are blessed in order to go forth and be a blessing in the world (Gen. 12:2). And notice that the pastor doesn't necessarily get the last word—the rubrics suggest that a deacon or ruling elder may speak the charge as an expression of their leadership in the congregation's service and common life.

BAPTISM AND REAFFIRMATION

Glory to God includes liturgies for the Sacrament of Baptism and the Reaffirmation of the Baptismal Covenant. The latter is especially for "persons who were baptized as infants and nurtured in the church, and who now are making a public profession of faith" (i.e., confirmation). In the early church, baptism, confirmation, and first communion were one and the same event. The rise of infant baptism and the requirement that a bishop be present to preside at confirmation (difficult in rural areas) led to the fragmentation of Christian initiation into three separate events. The liturgy in *Glory to God* (following the *BCW*) seeks to restore a sense of the unity of Christian initiation by presenting confirmation as a reaffirmation of the baptismal covenant.

The Sacrament of Baptism

The liturgy for Baptism begins with the Great Commission: to make disciples of all nations, baptizing them in the name of the triune God and teaching them to obey Jesus' commandments (Matt. 28:19–20). Not only is this statement the biblical "mandate" for baptism; it also shows us how the sacrament is connected with the church's mission. Responsive sentences of Scripture follow, expressing the theme of Christian unity in Baptism; these may be led by an ecumenical representative or a member of the congregation. A ruling elder presents the candidate(s) for Baptism, demonstrating the session's role in authorizing the sacrament and providing for the formation of the people of God. After inquiring about the candidate's (or parents') intent, the pastor addresses sponsors (if applicable) and the congregation, seeking their commitment in the ongoing support and nurture of the one(s) being baptized.

The Profession of Faith consists of two parts—first turning *away* from sin (the renunciation of evil), then turning *toward* God in Christ (the affirmation of faith). In the early church, this movement in the liturgy sometimes involved literal turning—first facing the western darkness (where the sun sets), then facing the eastern light (where the sun rises). The Apostles' Creed, traditionally associated with Baptism, is used as the Affirmation of Faith; it may be spoken in unison or led in a question-and-answer format ("Do you believe in God?"). The contemporary, ecumenical version of the creed is provided here, as a witness to our baptism into the universal church.

As with the eucharistic prayer in the Service for the Lord's Day, a full text for the Thanksgiving Over the Water is not provided; rather, rubrics explain the structure of the prayer and outline essential elements—giving thanks for God's faithfulness in salvation history, remembering Jesus' baptism, and praying for the power of the Holy Spirit—ending with praise to the triune God.

Rubrics indicate that the act of baptism may involve immersion or pouring water on the candidate's head; in any case, the application of water should be visible and generous enough to convey the extravagant grace of God. The use of Christian (first) names in baptism demonstrates the equality and kinship of the baptized—as children of God we are "on a first-name basis" in the body of Christ; symbols of status and other allegiances dissolve in the water of the font. The use of the triune name of God—Father, Son, and Holy Spirit—shows that we are baptized into the life of the one who created, redeemed, and sustains us. After the baptism, the laying on of hands signifies the gift of the Holy Spirit, by whom we are claimed as children of God and anointed for ministry in Christ's name. Anointing with oil may follow—another sign of the gift of the Spirit.

Next, those who have been baptized are welcomed into the life and fellowship of the church. It is especially appropriate for a ruling elder or ecumenical representative to issue this welcome. Candles, lighted from the church's paschal candle, may be given as a sign of the light of Christ. The sharing of Christ's peace reflects reconciliation and new relationship in the community of faith. The Service for the Lord's Day then continues with the Prayers of the People, including special petitions for those who have been baptized. The ancient pattern of Christian initiation is most fully expressed when the Eucharist can follow Baptism, with those who are baptized coming first to the table. If the congregation does not celebrate the Lord's Supper every Sunday, Baptisms should be scheduled on the first Sunday of the month (or another Sunday when the feast is kept).

Reaffirmation of the Baptismal Covenant

The structure of the liturgy for the reaffirmation of the baptismal covenant is, appropriately, parallel to that of the Sacrament of Baptism. A ruling elder presents the candidates for reaffirmation of baptism, and the pastor summarizes the journey of faith that has brought them to this place. A member of the congregation or ecumenical representative speaks sentences of Scripture, acknowledging the candidates' membership in the household of God. The renunciation of evil and affirmation of faith follow, again using the Apostles' Creed traditionally connected with Baptism. In this case, the prayer over the water acknowledges that the candidate has been previously baptized, and calls for the renewal and continuation of that covenant. Since this liturgy assumes that Baptism has already taken place, the decisive elements of water and the triune name of God are not present; the laying on of hands and anointing with oil, however, are repeated. A ruling elder welcomes those who have reaffirmed the baptismal covenant into full and mature participation in the mission and ministry of the church, and the peace of Christ is shared.

DAILY PRAYER

Glory to God provides four services for Daily Prayer: Morning, Midday, Evening, and Close of Day. The rhythm of Daily Prayer represented here is one that spans millennia, with ties to the worship of ancient Israel, the habits of Jesus, the teaching of the apostles, and the daily office of Christian monasticism. In contemporary practice, this pattern of devotion, study, and intercession continues to offer shape and substance for spiritual life—whether in personal or family settings, small-group gatherings, conferences, retreats, or councils of the church.

Although the four services differ somewhat in their content and structure, the "basic ingredients" are always the same: psalms (ideally sung), Scripture readings, and prayer. Each service begins with sentences of Scripture and ends with a dismissal and sign of peace. Psalms and Scripture readings may be drawn from a lectionary, such as the two-year daily lectionary of the *BCW* or the Revised Common Lectionary daily readings. A nonbiblical reading, such as an excerpt from the *Book of Confessions*, may also be read. Prayers of thanksgiving are offered for the many gifts of God we experience each day; prayers of intercession are spoken for the church, world, community, and personal concerns. The thanksgivings and intercessions end with a concluding collect and the Lord's Prayer.

A distinctive feature of the service for Evening Prayer is the (optional) singing of the *Phos Hilaron*, an ancient hymn to Christ the light, and a prayer of thanksgiving for the gift of light; the lighting of candles and/or the burning of incense (with the singing of Psalm 141) may be included. The liturgy for prayer at the Close of Day includes the element of confession—an opportunity to examine the struggles and failings of the day and ask for God's grace. Certain canticles—sung following the reading of Scripture—are associated with services of Daily Prayer: the Song of Zechariah (Luke 1:68–79) at Morning Prayer, the Song of Mary (Luke 1:46–55) at Evening Prayer, and the Song of Simeon (Luke 2:29–32) at the Close of Day.

OTHER TEXTS FOR WORSHIP

Following the liturgies for daily prayer, *Glory to God* includes a set of "other texts for worship." These texts are included because of their theological and historical significance, as well as their frequent use in worship. They are provided in three translations—English, Spanish, and Korean—reflecting the primary languages spoken in the Presbyterian Church (U.S.A.).

The first of these texts is the Nicene Creed. Drafted in the fourth century by a council convened by the emperor Constantine, the Nicene Creed is one of the earliest Christian affirmations of faith. It is also the most ecumenical—shared by Eastern Orthodox, Roman Catholic, and Protestant Christians around the world. Because of its ancient and ecumenical character, the Nicene Creed is traditionally spoken when the church celebrates the Eucharist. Note that only one version of the Nicene Creed is provided in *Glory to God*, since the PC(USA) has adopted the contemporary, common version as its official translation of the creed.

The next three texts—the Apostles' Creed, Lord's Prayer, and the Law of God—have been the bedrock of Christian formation in the Western church for at least sixteen centuries. Sermons from early church leaders indicate that new believers were expected to study and memorize these three texts before they could be received as members of Christ's body through Baptism. The Heidelberg and Westminster Catechisms are constructed as expositions of the creed, prayer, and commandments. Since the contemporary, ecumenical versions of the Apostles' Creed and Lord's Prayer were provided earlier, this section includes the more familiar, archaic texts. A listing of the Ten Commandments (based on Exodus 20) is provided, along with Jesus' summary of the law in Matthew 22 (citing Deut. 6:5 and Lev. 19:18).

The final piece in this collection of "other texts" is the Brief Statement of Faith of the Presbyterian Church (U.S.A.). This new creedal statement was composed to commemorate the 1983 reunion of the United Presbyterian Church in the

United States of America and the Presbyterian Church in the United States. The publication of *Glory to God* coincides with the thirtieth anniversary of that event. Major sections of the Brief Statement are numbered in order to facilitate the use of excerpts as Affirmations of Faith.

GLORY TO GOD

The liturgical texts found in the first fifty pages of *Glory to God* are just a beginning—they provide a firm foundation for "traditional, contemporary, ecumenical, and Reformed" worship, but they will need to be supplemented with materials for the seasons and festivals of the Christian year, liturgies for marriage and funerals, ordinations and installations, services of wholeness and healing, and so on. Fortunately, we have strong guidance and excellent resources for such occasions in the DFW and the *BCW*. Still, we hope and pray that these offerings will edify the church and enliven its worship as, together, we give glory to God.

Chapter 7

DECISIONS ABOUT LANGUAGE IN *GLORY TO GOD*

"Did you go changing the words?" Few questions posed to hymnal committees are as frequent or pointed as this one. And rightly so. From childhood forward, we learn about God through stories and songs, and we form deep-rooted attachments to texts that have nurtured our lives of faith. So if we are singing by heart a long-cherished hymn only to discover that people around us are singing different words from *Glory to God*, we may find ourselves perplexed.

TAMPERING WITH ORIGINALS

Thus word changes in hymns understandably provoke criticism. One line of critique goes something like this: "Hymnal committees should not tamper with texts; we should sing the words the way the authors wrote them." This protest implies that a hymn's original author is most probably a superior poet to members of an editorial board, and as such, his or her word choices should be left intact.

While such a critique has merit, it fails to take a few things into account. Most importantly, the words we think of as an author's "original" may simply be the text we grew up singing and therefore assume (incorrectly) to have precedence over any other version. In some such instances, to return from what we are *accustomed* to singing to what the author *actually* wrote would elicit stronger objections. Who among us would not balk at singing, "Draw nigh, draw nigh, Emmanuel" as an Advent hymn? Yet those are the words written by John Mason Neale to translate a medieval Latin text we now sing as "O Come, O Come, Emmanuel" (#88). Who at Christmas would be able to sing, "Hark how all the welkin rings!" without stumbling? Yet these are Charles Wesley's original words, only later adapted to speak of "herald angels" (#119).

Who among us would not balk at singing, "Draw nigh, draw nigh, Emmanuel" as an Advent hymn?

Such examples are not simply exceptions. In fact, the long-standing *norm* for hymnal editors has been to adapt texts to make them more singable and comprehensible for their intended audiences. Sometimes, for example, altering the word order of a text makes its accents fit more smoothly with its appointed melody: John Mason Neale's Palm Sunday hymn "All Glory, Laud, and Honor" (#196) is a case in point, since singing Neale's original version, "Glory and Laud and Honor," to the tune VALET WILL ICH DIR GEBEN, would put undue stress on the weaker syllable of the first word, "glo-RY."[1] Sometimes an author's original hymn contains terms not in the accustomed vocabulary of a group of singers, so revisions are made not to *cause* but to *prevent* verbal stumbling.

Another text from Neale is illustrative: his translation of an early Latin poem into the hymn "Christ Is Made the Sure Foundation" (#394) initially included a doxology praising the God who is "consubstantial, co-eternal, while unending ages run." The editors of *Hymns Ancient and Modern* in 1861 changed these adjectives to "one in might and one in glory,"[2] which is the text we still sing today.

PROCEED WITH CAUTION

Changing words must be done with caution, since shifts in vocabulary can also mean shifts in theology. However, sometimes theological shifts are the very reasons for revision. Two texts by Charles Wesley give pertinent examples. The second stanza of his "Love Divine, All Loves Excelling" (#366) has undergone numerous alterations by editors (including his own brother John) who were uncomfortable with the text's extreme view of Christian perfectibility in this life. "Take away our *power* of sinning" has thus become, "Take away the *love* of sinning."[3] In like manner, an eighteenth-century editor disagreed with the universalism implied in a line of Wesley's Easter hymn, "Christ the Lord Is Risen Today!" (#245): "Dying once, he all doth save." The line was amended to, "Once he died, our souls to save."[4] Subsequent editors have eliminated the word "once," making the line simply, "Jesus died, our souls to save," which is the version both in *The Presbyterian Hymnal* (1990) and in *Glory to God*.

Since textual revision is a far more normal practice than most people in the pews realize, those who insist we should sing hymns "the way the authors wrote them" might fruitfully explore how familiar they really are with authors' original phrasing. Below are a few fill-in-the-blank exercises to assist such exploration. (Answers appear at the end of the chapter.)

- "Alas! And Did My Savior Bleed,"[5] Isaac Watts (#212)
  - Stanza 1: "Would he [Christ] devote that sacred head / for _____ as I!"
  - Stanza 3: "Well might the sun in darkness hide / and shut its glories in, / when _____ died . . ."
- "For the Beauty of the Earth,"[6] Folliott Sandford Pierpoint (#14)
  - Refrain: "_____ to thee we raise / this our _____."
- "Rock of Ages, Cleft for Me,"[7] Augustus M. Toplady (#438)
  - Stanza 1: "Be of sin the double cure, / _____."
  - Stanza 4: "While I draw this fleeting breath, / when my _____ in death . . ."

THE DISTINCTIVENESS OF HYMN POETRY

Even faced with such examples of how revision has been used throughout the centuries, a critic might still object that "is" does not equal "ought": just because something *has* been done need not imply that it *should* be done. A purist might continue to argue that we should leave poets' original words untouched—unless we can make a clear case that hymn poems differ in fundamental ways from other kinds of poetry.

No less an authority than Louis Fitzgerald Benson makes this case. Editor of the Presbyterian *Hymnal* of 1895 (and its subsequent revisions in 1911 and 1917), Benson's meticulous scholarship set the professional standard for generations of hymnal editors to come. In a book on *The Hymnody of the Christian Church*, he aptly observed, "In a collection of poems for poetry's sake the rule of fidelity of text is absolute. In a collection of hymns for congregational use, fidelity must be tempered by considerations of practical utility."[8]

This point is crucial. Hymns are not "poems for poetry's sake." The hymn poem does not exist to call attention to its own artistry, but rather to point beyond itself to the artistry of God. As *functional* rather than *pure* art, hymns are less like oil paintings in a museum (where the "rule of fidelity" to the original might well be absolute) and more like sweaters hand-knitted to offer warmth when the weather grows cold. While sweaters, like hymns, can be beautifully crafted, they ultimately have a job to do. If over the years of doing that job they show signs of fraying, it is far from blasphemous to darn a careful repair over the worn spot. In like manner, if a hymn text contains words that have grown puzzling or problematic through shifts in vocabulary (like "consubstantial" in an example above), if it causes singers to stumble over syllables that do not fit the meter of a tune, or, more significantly, if it contains concepts that do not fit the theology of their context, then it is no longer able to do its job of facilitating worship as effectively as it might.

These are the "considerations of practical utility" that Benson had in mind. A few years before his death, looking back over his long career, he actually faulted himself for making "too little use of the privilege of amendment" in the collections he compiled, operating instead out of an "overscrupulosity" with regard to original texts. "With more than thirty years of added experience," he remarked, "I should now not hesitate to go much further."[9] He could say this not simply as an editor but as a poet as well. Presbyterian hymnals are still enriched by his "O Sing a Song of Bethlehem" (#159) and "For the Bread Which You Have Broken" (#516). We might imagine that far from objecting that his original language had been tampered with in shifting from "thou hast" to "you have" in the latter of these examples, Benson would appreciate the fact that his words from a prior century are being kept current for new generations of singers.

THE COMMITTEE'S PRINCIPLES

Still, permission to exercise Benson's "privilege of amendment" is not license to alter words heedlessly or haphazardly. Thus, when approaching the task of creating a twenty-first-century collection of hymns for both old and new generations of singers, the Presbyterian Committee on Congregational Song (PCOCS) began by drafting "A Statement on Language" to guide their efforts. This statement is included here as chapter 8. In seeking principles of operation, however, we quickly realized that no "one-size-fits-all" editorial model would work. Decisions about language would ultimately have to be made on a case-by-case basis, attentive to "issues of tradition, theological integrity, poetic quality, and copyright."[10]

> We worked hard to find common texts that we might sing in unity with sisters and brothers in churches within our ecumenical partnership.

Our language concerns were not simply about gender pronouns, as some might imagine, but about larger issues regarding the fit of texts to tunes and to our contemporary theological and social context. In the latter regard, for example, we worked hard to find common texts that we might sing in unity with sisters and brothers in churches within our ecumenical partnership. Given our shared beliefs as Christians, it is remarkable that words sung across denominations have come to be so different, even when we are presumably voicing the "same" hymn! In an era when people who join Presbyterian congregations are more likely than ever to have grown up in some different tradition, it is increasingly desirable to find ways that we can come together to sing, metaphorically if not literally, off the same page.

Beyond such concerns for commonality, our verbal concerns focused on three key areas: archaic, prejudicial, and gendered language.

ARCHAIC LANGUAGE

Just as the Reformers insisted on translating the Bible from Latin into the languages people actually spoke, so hymnal editors have frequently attempted to rephrase hymns in something closer to the spoken idioms of their own day. The *Worship Book* of 1975 was a pioneer in such efforts in the Presbyterian Church, even rendering "I Greet Thee Who My Sure Redeemer Art" as "We Greet You, Sure Redeemer from All Strife." The Presbyterian Committee on Congregational Song took more of a middle ground on this issue, electing to return the text attributed to Calvin to its more familiar form and generally opting not to alter pronouns in familiar first lines or in stanzas where words like "thee" or "thine" occupied rhyming positions.

We did, however, shift occasional archaic words into more contemporary vocabulary in places where the shift seemed unlikely to cause an awkward tension between what some might be singing by heart and what others were singing off the page. With hymnal editors before us, we made such occasional revisions out of a desire to keep hymns in an idiom whereby they speak to and from our own condition. After all, one test of a good hymn is that it voices a prayer we might utter ourselves if we had the verbal skill of the author. Again, hymns are not intended as museum pieces or relics of a bygone era but as the living voice of contemporary believers.

PREJUDICIAL LANGUAGE

Because many beloved hymns do hail from earlier historic eras, they do not always manifest sensitivity to language that has come to be seen as biased or stereotyping in our day. Thus, for example, working with the Office of Disability Concerns, the PCOCS attempted to avoid verbal constructions implying that physical disabilities such as sight, hearing, or mobility impairments are evidence of moral failing. The 1990 hymnal committee had already begun this editorial work. It is a delicate task, however, since powerful biblical metaphors speak of the messianic age as a time when the blind will see, the deaf will hear, and the lame will walk. *Glory to God* preserves some such images as expressive of our deep hope for personal and cosmic healing. In other instances, however, authors of recent texts proved willing to work with us in revising their works to be less unintentionally prejudicial.

In making changes for reasons of potential prejudice, we were aware that some critics would charge us with "political correctness." On further reflection, however, such a charge is puzzling. After all, it is not from the *political* arena that we learn the importance of putting our neighbors' needs above our own. From a Christian perspective, surely the sacrifice of a particular familiar word seems a small price to pay for the purpose of helping all our sisters and brothers feel welcomed and valued: hospitality toward the other and the stranger expresses *biblical*, not political, correctness. Indeed, it constitutes an arena in which we might take pleasure in our efforts to "outdo one another in showing honor" (Rom. 12:10).

GENDERED LANGUAGE

Critics, however, are also apt to voice the charge of political correctness in cases where hymnal committees alter gender-specific references. Again, though, if as Christians we take to heart teachings about hospitality, then even if masculine pronouns do not bother us personally, might we not be willing to show biblical correctness in putting the feelings of others above our own? For some members of our church family, exclusively male language sounds like a painful reinforcement of discriminatory social systems—social systems that Jesus himself upended in treating men and women as persons of equal worth.

As with archaic language, so with gendered language the PCOCS attempted a mediating position. Our Statement on Language expresses a clear preference for inclusive language regarding human beings. So, for instance, "Men of faith, rise up and sing" (#319) is balanced by a second stanza that calls for "women of the truth" to rise up as well. A version of Psalm 133, "O Look and Wonder" (#397) sings in one stanza of how good it is when brothers dwell in peace with one another, and in subsequent stanzas it tells of the joy of unity among sisters and "all earth's people." While we made an editorial decision not to insert any *new* asterisks into *Glory to God* to provide alternate, inclusive-language versions of texts, where asterisks appeared in the 1990 hymnal, we left them in place. So, for example, "Dear Lord and Father of Mankind" (#169) continues to offer another option for singers in place of the mankind reference ("Dear Lord, Creator good and kind").

In approaching God-language, we exercised even more caution than when assessing language for humans. The PCOCS Statement on Language acknowledges:

> While many are deeply nurtured and comforted by traditional imagery for God, many others are concerned about associations of patriarchy and other forms of domination and are looking for other and more diverse language.[11]

Recognizing, therefore, that our hymnal is intended for a vast body of believers whose positions on such questions differ, we adopted a policy of expansive language for God. In other words, the full array of biblical metaphors for God is retained, including references to God as Father, Lord, and King. But also in this array appear images in which God is the "womb of life and source of being" (#3) and the "mothering" one who gave us birth (#7). There are also images that have no gendered connotations at all: "Source and Sovereign, Rock and Cloud" (#11), "fiery pillar" (#315), "Rock of Ages" (#438), and many, many more.

THE LAST WORD

In any hymn about God, our Statement on Language reminds us, we are attempting to sing of "the one whose ways and thoughts are as beyond human speech as the heaven is higher than the earth (Isa. 55:8–9)."[12] Hence *none* of our words—whether an author's originals or a committee's alterations—can ever be fully adequate. Yet drawing on God's revelation in Scripture to test the spirits of any human creation or re-creation, we do our best to sing boldly and faithfully. Glory to God!

ANSWERS TO
FILL-IN-THE-BLANK EXERCISES

- Watts, Stanza 1: "for such a worm as I"; when God the mighty maker died."
- Watts, Staza 3: "Christ our God to thee we raise / this, our sacrifice of praise."
- Pierpoint, Refrain: "Lord of all . . ." and ". . . hymn of grateful praise."
- Toplady, Stanza 1: Toplady himself wrote two versions: initially, "save from wrath and make me pure," which he later revised to "save me from its guilt and power" (the

latter being preferred in Presbyterian, and the former in Methodist and Baptist hymnals).
– Toplady, Stanza 4: "when my eye-strings break in death."

NOTES

1. *Companion to the Hymnal,* ed. Fred Gealy, Austin Lovelace, and Carlton Young (Nashville: Abingdon, 1970), 74.
2. Ibid., 131.
3. Ibid., 281.
4. Ibid., 133.
5. Ibid., 71.
6. Ibid., 180.
7. Ibid., 364.
8. Louis F. Benson, *The Hymnody of the Christian Church* (Richmond, VA: John Knox Press, 1956), 211.
9. Ibid., 218.
10. "A Statement on Language," in *Glory to God* (Louisville, KY: Wetminster John Knox Press, 2013), 929.
11. Ibid., 928.
12. Ibid.

Chapter 8

A STATEMENT ON LANGUAGE

Language is close to the heart of Christian faith. As befits a faith community called into being by a God we know as the Word made flesh, we pray, proclaim, teach, comfort, admonish, serve, and administer justice with words woven in and through all our actions. Language used in worship has great power. Therefore the language used in collections of hymns, psalms, and spiritual songs matters a great deal. Worshipful words joined to worshipful music deeply shape the faith and practices of the church.

The church has been enriched by several decades of conversations about language used for God and for the people of God. Christians in denominations like the Presbyterian Church (U.S.A.) have become aware that our language can exclude and stereotype, but also that carefully chosen language can embrace and include people who have been separated from the centers of power. A commitment to inclusive language for the people of God reflects the consensus of the church.[1] When it comes to language used for God, however, the conversation is still ongoing. While many are deeply nurtured and comforted by traditional imagery for God, many others are concerned about associations of patriarchy and other forms of domination and are looking for other and more diverse language.

> Christians in denominations like the Presbyterian Church (U.S.A.) have become aware that our language can exclude and stereotype, but also that carefully chosen language can embrace and include people who have been separated from the centers of power.

In negotiating these different convictions, the Presbyterian Committee on Congregational Song is guided by the theological framework of this new collection of songs: salvation history. Scripture uses an abundantly rich array of prose and poetry to tell us about God's powerful acts of creation, redemption, and final transformation. Much biblical imagery is indeed masculine, but there is also a wide variety of other metaphors that are either feminine or gender-neutral. Most important, behind all biblical narrative lies the deep and prevailing sense that God is the one whose ways and thoughts are as beyond human speech as the heaven is higher than the earth (Isa. 55:8–9). Our lips need to be cleansed by a burning coal before we speak or sing any word about the holy God (Isa. 6:5).

The framework of salvation history requires a collection of songs that reflects the full extent of the biblical narrative and also the full array of biblical language used for God—even if that leads us to using words and imagery that go beyond our natural comfort.

Given these commitments, the committee seeks a songbook that is characterized, as a church document formulates it, by "inclusive language with reference to the people of God, and expansive language with reference to God."[2] Thus the committee uses the following guidelines:

Language used for the people of God

- Language that stereotypes persons according to categories such as gender, race, ethnicity, socioeconomic class, sexual orientation, age, or disabilities will be avoided.
- The "generic masculine" is no longer universally understood to include persons of both genders and will therefore be avoided. Texts that employ the generic masculine will be evaluated individually to determine what alterations, if any, are poetically appropriate.
- Salvation history invites us to sing joyfully of the creative and healing presence of our God. We will be sensitive, however, to potentially denigrating implications of poetic metaphors in our songs, especially with respect to persons of color or with disabilities.

Language used for God

- The collection will draw from the full reservoir of biblical imagery for God and God's gracious acts. The final product will include both metaphors that are comfortable in their familiarity and those that are enriching in their newness.
- The collection will emphasize that the God who meets us so graciously and intimately in salvation history is at the same time one who is wholly other and beyond gender.[3] Therefore, texts will reflect a strong preference for avoiding the use of male pronouns for God. In evaluating each hymn or song, issues of tradition, theological integrity, poetic quality, and copyright will all be considered. The goal is a collection in which traditional hymns

and songs are balanced with others that are more gender-neutral or expansive in their reference to God.

> The goal is a collection in which traditional hymns and songs are balanced with others that are more gender-neutral or expansive in their reference to God.

- Two references to God should be preserved in the collection:

  1. In the biblical narrative both the God of Israel and Christ are called "Lord." The practice of calling God "Lord" goes back to Greek-speaking Jews who sought to avoid pronouncing God's holy name, YHWH, by using a replacement term: Lord (*Kyrios*). The practice has since been followed by virtually all Christian Bible translations. Rather than being an expression of domination or masculinity, "Lord" stands in for the name by which God chose to disclose Godself in Hebrew Scripture (Exod. 3:15).

     That "Jesus Christ is Lord (*Kyrios*)" is one of the oldest confessions concerning Jesus. It has both a Roman and a Jewish background. On the one hand, "Lord" (*Kyrios*) was the title of the Roman emperor. When the writers of the New Testament confess Jesus to be Lord, they thereby proclaim that not Caesar, but Christ rules this world. On the other hand, in applying the reference to the name of Israel's God to Jesus, the New Testament makes a startling identity statement: that in Jesus this very God has become present among us.

     Were we no longer to use "Lord" for Israel's God, we would no longer understand what we claim about Jesus' identity when we confess him Lord. Were we no longer to use "Lord" for Jesus, we would lose the strongest defense we have against empire: that Christ is Lord, and not Caesar.

2. The church confesses a Trinitarian God: one God, in Father, Son, and Holy Spirit. This is the formula by which we are baptized; this is the name that unites us with each other and with all Christian communities beyond our denomination (Matt. 28:19). This threefold name will not be eliminated. At the same time, many other images and metaphors for the Trinity will be welcomed, as long as they express the principles of Trinitarian theology:

a. God exists in three persons, but there is nevertheless only one God who knows and loves and acts;

b. in salvation history, no person of the Trinity acts alone; every act is an act of all three persons in the one God;

c. each person of the Trinity is not a part of God, but fully God.

—Ratified by the Presbyterian Committee on Congregational Song (PCOCS), October 2009

NOTES

1. Cf. the *Book of Order*, the PC(USA) "Report and Recommendations in Response to Referral on Inclusive Language" (1985), and the "Report to the Church on Issues of Language and Gender" (2000).

2. *Well Chosen Words!* Published and revised by the Women's Ministries, National Ministries Division, and the Advocacy Committee for Women's Concerns, a ministry of the Presbyterian Mission Agency of the PC(USA), 2012. Cf. also the *Book of Order*.

3. Cf. the 1998 PC(USA) *The Study Catechism*, questions 11–13.

Chapter 9

MUSICAL GENRES IN *GLORY TO GOD*

What do "Glory Be to the Father" (#581), "Glory to God, Whose Goodness Shines on Me" (#582), and "Glory to God (*Gloria a Dios*)" (#585) have in common? They are adaptations of the traditional Gloria Patri text set in three different musical styles: a traditional four-part hymn setting, a rousing gospel song, and a rhythmic global setting. *Glory to God* is a resource replete with texts and tunes from varied traditions that give our worship voice. In chapter 6, "Liturgy in *Glory to God*," David Gambrell described the worship resources in our new hymnal as "simultaneously traditional, contemporary, ecumenical, and Reformed—or to put it another way: 'old, new, borrowed, and blue'" (p. 46). The same description applies to the musical resources in *Glory to God,* a collection of hymns, psalms, and spiritual songs drawn from sources spanning two thousand years of Christian worship. This chapter will survey seven distinct musical styles used throughout *Glory* to God and suggest practical applications in singing liturgical responses from the "Service Music" section.

STREAMS OF SONG

The Presbyterian Committee on Congregational Song (PCOCS) carried forward more than 65 percent of the content from *The Presbyterian Hymnal* (1990) to *Glory to God,* leaving space for a generous number of additional hymns, psalms, and spiritual songs chosen from among ten thousand selections reviewed for inclusion. Some songs are old favorites borrowed from other hymnals; some are contemporary praise music; some are new texts set as traditional hymns; others are songs from ecumenical and global communities; and some are psalms from our Reformed heritage. Whether old, new, borrowed, or blue, there is a wide spectrum of musical styles represented.

In order to understand and manage this astounding number of available selections, the committee used a model developed by Michael Hawn called "Streams of Song," a useful, overarching organizational metaphor for current congregational song. Rather than describing a tune or text as traditional or contemporary, with all the connotations those terms can carry, Hawn suggests that the vast repertoire of congregational song available today can be understood as coming from different streams of the church. Hawn writes:

> Streams have a source, and each of the proposed seven streams of song comes from particular sources of faith—a particular expression of piety. Streams come in various widths and depths. Not all streams are the same. Some of the song streams are rushing and seem to be overflowing their banks because of the musical outpouring generated from their particular piety source. Others are steady in their flow, and yet others may be either drying up or merging with other

streams. Streams meander; they do not flow in straight lines like canals. They occasionally crisscross each other. . . . Some songs fit comfortably in two or more streams.

This fluid model stands in contrast to a pigeonhole approach where everything is organized neatly. The fluidity of this model reflects how these songs usually appear in hymnals—songs from one tradition organized around a particular season of the Christian year or theological theme are placed in juxtaposition to other streams. Hymns demonstrate flexibility in their liturgical possibilities. . . .

Finally, streams are vibrant parts of creation, carrying us along with them, offering constant changes in depth, rate of flow and character.[1]

These seven streams, accounting for most of the congregational song in *Glory to God*, are:

1. Roman Catholic Liturgical Renewal
2. Classic Contemporary Protestant Hymnody
3. The African American Stream
4. Gospel and Revival Songs
5. Folk Hymnody
6. Pentecostal Song
7. Ecumenical and Global Stream[2]

Hawn's model frees us from the need to pigeonhole text or music as traditional or contemporary, old or new, permitting our songs to flow freely from all the streams.

NAVIGATING THE STREAMS: AN OVERVIEW

This model is useful for viewing historical hymns of our faith juxtaposed with newer expressions and implies something about musical style. Below is a brief description of each stream and its origin, with illustrative examples found in *Glory to God*.

Stream One: Roman Catholic Liturgical Renewal reflects reform set forth by Vatican II involving music for sacraments, responsorial psalms, lectionary, Christian year, and rituals. Since the mid-1960s, Protestant collections have borrowed heavily from this stream of song.

> Hawn's model frees us from the need to pigeonhole text or music as traditional or contemporary, old or new, permitting our songs to flow freely from all the streams.

The headwaters forming this stream include some of the church's oldest sung texts that Presbyterians continue to sing: "Creator of the Stars of Night" (#84), "O Come, O Come, Emmanuel" (#88), and "Of the Father's Love Begotten" (#108).[3] They are set to plainsong (chant) and sung in unison. Recent hymns from the Roman Catholic Liturgical Renewal, such as "You Who Dwell in the Shelter of the Lord" (#43), "I, the Lord of Sea and Sky" (#69), "One Bread, One Body" (#530), and "Seed, Scattered and Sown" (#531) typically feature stanzas sung by a cantor or leader with a unison refrain sung by the congregation. In practice, a small ensemble or choir can sing the stanzas, with the congregation joining on the refrain. Using a cantor or ensemble on the stanzas is especially helpful when teaching the congregation one of these new songs. Organ, piano, or guitar provide satisfactory accompaniment.

Stream Two: Classic Contemporary Protestant Hymnody surges from the "hymnic explosion" that began in Great Britain in the 1960s and spread to other English-speaking countries. This large, steady stream features strophic texts, new metrical psalm settings, Scripture paraphrases, and prophetic hymns on justice themes.[4] Hymn writers such as Mary Louise Bringle, Ruth Duck, Fred Pratt Green, Shirley Erena Murray, Thomas

Troeger, and Brian Wren are a few of the many contributors to this stream.

Early texts in this stream include hymns by various Reformers, Isaac Watts, and the Wesleys. Standards such as "Holy, Holy, Holy! Lord God Almighty!" (#1), "Guide Me, O Thou Great Jehovah" (#65), "When I Survey the Wondrous Cross" (#223), "All Hail the Power of Jesus' Name!" (#263), and "O for a Thousand Tongues to Sing" (#610) are sung in traditional four-part arrangements with organ or piano accompaniment.

New Classic Contemporary Protestant Hymnody texts are frequently paired with a familiar tune, making the hymn quickly accessible for a congregation. For example, "Go to the World!" (#295) is set to the tune SINE SOMINE ("For All the Saints") and "God Is Calling through the Whisper" (#410) is sung to W ŻŁOBIE LEŻY ("Infant Lowly, Infant Holy"). Other hymn texts are paired with fresh, new tunes that can accommodate strophic texts. While many of the new melodies still appear in traditional four-voice settings, some are intended for unison singing, such as the ballad-style "God the Sculptor of the Mountains" (#5), "Ten Lepers Facing Constant Scorn" (#179), "When at This Table" (#537), or "God, Be the Love to Search and Keep Me" (#543). In addition to organ or piano accompaniment, guitar can be effective with many of these melodies.

Stream Three: The African American Stream is found in virtually all Christian traditions with spirituals and gospel hymns that relate biblical stories in a context of faith and hope amid adversity. Its precursors include anonymous spirituals and slave songs.[5] The spirituals frequently employ a call-and-response text, that is, the first and second lines are the same and are followed by a refrain, as in "Were You There" (#228) and "We Shall Overcome" (#379). Over time, the African American community supplemented spirituals with gospel hymns that featured rich harmonies unfolding expansively, as in "Hark!

The Herald Angels Sing" (#127) and "Soon and Very Soon" (#384). Whether accompanied by keyboard instruments, guitar, or band, these hymns require a relaxed tempo so that all may savor the experience.

Stream Four: Gospel and Revival Songs includes songs and hymns of salvation and personal religious experience. These songs, products of the eighteenth- and nineteenth-century revivals and Sunday School era, were penned by writers such as Fanny Crosby and tunesmiths such as William Bradbury. Although these songs continued to flourish in the twentieth century, Hawn observes that this stream appears to be merging with streams three and six, which have texts that also focus on salvation and personal experience.[6]

Songs brought forward from *The Presbyterian Hymnal* (1990) include gospel and Sunday-school era songs such as "Jesus Loves Me" (#188) and "To God Be the Glory" (#634). Gospel and Revival Songs new to *Glory to God* include "Shall We Gather at the River" (#375), "Softly and Tenderly Jesus Is Calling" (#418), "I Love to Tell the Story" (#462), and "Why Should I Feel Discouraged?" (#661). Some gospel tunes are rousing and rhythmic while others feature tender, sentimental melodies. Most are in four-part harmony and are traditionally accompanied by piano and organ. The judicious addition of other instruments can enrich the singing.

Stream Five: Folk Hymnody has generally been an accepted part of the church's song and enjoyed resurgence in the 1960s with music from folk masses. *Glory to God* contains some early contributions, such as hymns from the singing school tradition, choruses, folk tunes, and rounds or canons.[7] Familiar early examples include "What Wondrous Love Is This" (#215) and the canon (round) "When Jesus Wept" (#194). Recent examples include "What Does the Lord Require of You?" (#70), "Spirit, Spirit of Gentleness" (#291), and "We Are One in the Spirit" (#300). Acoustic guitar accompaniment is a natural choice with much folk hymnody. Rounds/canons such as "What Does the Lord Require of You?" and "When Jesus Wept" are profoundly moving when sung unaccompanied (a cappella).

Stream Six: Pentecostal Song is a surging stream birthed in the early twentieth-century American Pentecostal movement. Within this stream there are various styles of texts and songs identified as praise choruses, Scripture songs, worship choruses, modern hymns, and adaptations of contemporary Christian music for congregations.[8] This stream, underrepresented in *The Presbyterian Hymnal* (1990), has been expanded in *Glory to God*. "Lord, the Light of Your Love Is Shining" (#192), "Men of Faith, Rise Up and Sing" (#319), "Open the Eyes of My Heart" (#452), and "Give Thanks" (#647) are several of the new additions from this stream. Many of these songs are composed in popular song form using a verse/refrain/bridge format. Piano and instrumental praise bands usually accompany these songs, although a capable organist can add support and color on the refrains.

Stream Seven: Ecumenical and Global Stream reflects texts and tunes contributed by Christians from around the world and includes songs from the ecumenical communities of Iona and Taizé. These songs offer wisdom from the larger church and enable us to join in song with Christians from every corner of the world. "If You Only Had Faith" (#176), "Filled with Excitement (*Mantos y palmas*)" (#199), "Christ Has Arisen, Alleluia" (#251), "Holy Lamb of God (*Ya hamalallah*)" (#602), "Sing Out, My Soul" (#646), and "We Are Marching in the Light of God (*Siyahamba*)" (#853) all emerge from this rich stream. Numerous global and ecumenical songs are short in length, making them useful for various places in the service as responses.[9] Musical styles are as varied as the cultures that birthed the songs. While much of this music is traditionally sung without instrumental accompaniment, indigenous instruments add new dimensions in sound.

Each stream is represented in *Glory to God* as this breakdown shows:

- 10% Roman Catholic Liturgical Renewal
- 58% Classic Contemporary Protestant Hymnody
- 4% The African American Stream
- 4% Gospel and Revival Songs
- 2% Folk Hymnody
- 5% Pentecostal Song
- 17% Ecumenical and Global Stream

SWIMMING THE STREAMS: SERVICE MUSIC

The gamut of musical style encompassed in *Glory to God* will engage the assembly in song regardless of their "native" musical language. The "Service Music" section of *Glory to God* (#551–#609) offers similar versatility in singing liturgical song. Expanded from the forty hymns in the 1990 hymnal to fifty-eight hymns, this section contains seven partial settings of eucharistic responses and thirty-five single responses.

The seven partial settings of the liturgy may include a Kyrie ("Lord, Have Mercy"), Sanctus ("Holy, Holy, Holy"), Memorial Acclamation ("Christ Has Died; Christ Is Risen"), and Amen. Most of these settings are based on a single tune, making them accessible and memorable for congregations. For example, the five responses in the setting by Richard Proulx (#551–#555) are based on the familiar American folk tune LAND OF REST, a tune also used for hymns #545, #691, and #796. Both Per Harling's set (#559–#561) and Proulx's adaptation of Franz Schubert's *Deutsche Messe* (#562–#564) offer four-part settings for a congregation or choir.

The following table shows the distribution of the service music in *Glory to God* by location in the stream of song model, title, and composer, illustrating that the responses for the liturgy are not limited to chants or staid settings.

Stream	Setting	Composer/ Arranger/Source
African American (Stream 3)	556-558 (Sanctus, Memorial Acclamation, Amen)	Leon Roberts
	600 Amen	Nelsie T. Johnson
Classic Contemporary Protestant Hymnody (Stream 2)	559-561 (Sanctus, Memorial Acclamation, Amen)	Thomas Pavlechko
	562-564 (Sanctus, Memorial Acclamation, Amen)	Per Harling
	572-574 (Sanctus, Memorial Acclamation, Amen)	Richard Proulx
	581 Gloria Patri	Henry W. Greatorex
	599 Amen	Johann G. Naumann
	601 Amen	Anonymous Danish
	608 Praise God, from Whom All Blessings Flow	Hal H. Hopson
	609 Praise God, from Whom All Blessings Flow	*Geistliche Kirchengesäng*
Ecumenical and Global Stream (Stream 7)	576 Lord, Have Mercy	Swee Hong Lim/Asian
	578 O Lord, Have Mercy	harm. Carlton R. Young/Guarani

Stream	Setting	Composer/ Arranger/Source
Ecumenical and Global Stream (Stream 7) (continued)	579 Lord, Have Mercy	Russian Orthodox chant
	580 Glory Be to the Father	Scottish chant
	583 Glory to God	Jacques Berthier/Taizé
	584 Glory, Glory, Glory	Pablo Sosa/Argentine
	585 Glory to God	Anonymous/Peruvian melody
	586 Alleluia	Jacques Berthier/Taizé
	587 Alleluia!	Fintan O'Carroll; harm. Christopher Walker/ Scottish
	589 Alleluia	Honduran melody
	590 Hallelujah	Abraham Maraire; arr. Patrick Matsikenyiri/ Zimbabwean
	591 Halle, Halle, Hallelujah!	arr. John L. Bell/Caribbean melody/Iona Community
	594 Holy, Holy, Holy, Holy	Guillermo Cuéllar; arr. Raquel Mora Martínez/El Salvadoran
	595 Holy, Holy, Holy	Traditional/Argentine
	596 You Are Holy	Per Harling
	597 Holy, Most Holy Lord	arr. Greg Scheer/South African
	598 Amen, We Praise Your Name	S. C. Molefe; transcr. David Dargie/South African

Stream	Setting	Composer/ Arranger/Source
Folk Hymnody (Stream 5)	551-555 (Kyrie, Sanctus, Memorial Acclamation, Amen, Agnus Dei)	Richard Proulx/American folk melody
	577 Lord, Have Mercy	Dinah Reindorf
Gospel, Revival, and Pentecostal Songs (Streams 4 and 6)	582 Glory to God, Whose Goodness Shines on Me	Paul M. Vasile
	592 Holy, Holy, Holy	Paul M. Vasile
	593 Holy, Holy	David E. Poole
	603 Lamb of God	Paul M. Vasile
Roman Catholic Liturgical Renewal (Stream 1)	565-568 (Sanctus, Memorial Acclamation 1 and 2, Amen)	Curt Oliver
	569-571 (Sanctus, Memorial Acclamation, Amen)	Howard Hughes
	588 Alleluia	Robert Buckley Farlee
	604 Lamb of God	Marty Haugen

The outline for "The Service for the Lord's Day" on pages 1–13 of *Glory to God* suggests places where service music can be used in the four-part worship structure of Gathering, Word, Eucharist, and Sending. While some congregations are accustomed to singing liturgical songs/responses throughout the service, other congregations are novices with this practice. The variety of musical styles in *Glory to God* is useful in either context.

Many Presbyterian congregations sing a Gloria Patri, often following the Assurance of Pardon. This is an excellent place to substitute a congregation's accustomed response with the gospel-style "Glory to God, Whose Goodness Shines on Me" (#582) or a response from the global church, such as "Glory to God (*Gloria a Dios*)" (#585). New tunes, new rhythms, and new instruments lend a fresh voice to the assembly's praise.

For a congregation experienced in singing responses during the Eucharist, the four-part settings by Harling and Proulx may satisfy or perhaps challenge their musical sensibilities. For congregations who are novices in this practice, learning a single response would serve as an excellent point of entry into this practice. For example, these words from the liturgy invite us to sing:

> Therefore we praise you,
> joining our voices with choirs of angels,
> with prophets, apostles, and martyrs,
> and with all the faithful of every time and place,
> who forever sing to the glory of your name.[10]

The assembly's Sanctus may be an exuberant explosion (#592), an intimate and awe-filled prayer (#593), or a robust gospel-style declaration (#556).

Encouraging congregations to sing from multiple streams requires thoughtful planning, good teaching, and strong musical leadership. The accompanist edition of *Glory to God* is an excellent resource for musicians, as it provides stylistically appropriate accompaniments and performance suggestions.

Encouraging congregations to sing from multiple streams requires thoughtful planning, good teaching, and strong musical leadership.

Every section in *Glory to God* offers us opportunities to sing from varied streams of faith and wade in different musical styles. Whether these streams are familiar and comfortable or disquieting and challenging, we need to sing the "old, new, borrowed, and blue" to keep us rooted in our Reformed tradition and to prod us into new ventures in faith.

NOTES

1. C. Michael Hawn, "Streams of Song: An Overview of Congregational Song in the Twenty-First Century," *The Hymn: A Journal of Congregational Song* 61, no. 1 (Winter 2010): 20.
2. Ibid., 20–21.
3. C. Michael Hawn, ed., *New Songs of Celebration Render* (Chicago: GIA, 2013), xxxi.
4. Ibid.
5. Ibid., xxxii.
6. Ibid.
7. Ibid.
8. Ibid., xxxiii.
9. Ibid.
10. *Book of Common Worship* (Louisville, KY: Westminster John Knox Press, 1993), 70.

Chapter 10

INTRODUCING *GLORY TO GOD* TO YOUR CHURCH

What is this book, purple and crimson,
chock full of notes both new and old:
metrical psalms, praise tunes, and hymns
on God's greatest stories ever told?
This is a book that helps us profess
to whom our lives belong
in liturgy and song.

Hymn parodies walk a tricky line: one person's "clever" is all too easily another person's "offensive." Where on this line would you put a plea for Lenten disciplines, modeled after Passover observances, titled "Just a Kosher Walk with Thee"? How about a song extolling the contributions of a new and much-needed male voice to the choir: "Amazing Bass, How Sweet the Sound"?

Less iffy, I suspect, than either of the above examples—perhaps because the text being parodied is less familiar—are the lines quoted above. "What Is This Book" mimics a text by Dutch pastor Huub Oosterhuis that was rendered into English by London-born teacher David Smith. Writing about the church, the author poses the question, "What is this place where we are meeting? / Only a house, the earth its floor. . . ." These words, as well as my parody of them, are set to a charming seventeenth-century Dutch tune, KOMT NU MET zang, which is appearing for the first time in a Presbyterian hymnal in *Glory to God*.

There are a number of important issues for worshipers first encountering *Glory to God* and for worship leaders facilitating its introduction. The purple or "crimson" hymnal is, indeed, "chock full of notes": not just musical notes, as would be expected in a song collection, but also verbal notes. Every hymn or song, with the exception of service music (sung liturgical texts such as Gloria or Kyrie), is annotated with a brief "program note" sharing something about the piece's history, authorship, music, or theology.

"Metrical psalms," both old and new, form an important part of the contents, honoring the fact that our forebears who worshiped in Calvin's Reformed tradition sang only psalms translated from their original linguistic forms into regularly metered, rhyming verse. "Hymns" by human rather than divinely inspired biblical authors were relative latecomers into the Presbyterian repertoire, although today they constitute a major component of our singing. Of even more recent vintage are "praise tunes" from the blossoming of contemporary Christian music in the late twentieth and early twenty-first centuries. Several time-tested examples of this genre have made their way into *Glory to God*, representing the rich diversity of modern worship styles.

> Our forebears . . . sang only psalms translated from their original linguistic forms into regularly metered, rhyming verse.

Whatever their vintage, all the songs included share a common focus on "God's greatest stories ever told." In fact, the ordering of hymns in *Glory to God* follows the outline of salvation history, beginning with the triune God who has been for all eternity; moving through God's creation of the world and care for its inhabitants in calling and covenant; continuing into anticipations of a coming messiah and the climactic events of the birth, life, death, and resurrection of Jesus; picking up again with the descent of the Spirit and formation of the church; and culminating in the looked-for return of Christ and the creation of a new heaven and a new earth. More about this organizing framework can be found in the theological vision statement written by the Presbyterian Committee on Congregational Song to guide our work (see chap. 5). *Glory to God* includes this statement as an appendix to the hymnal.

People accustomed to the liturgical-year structure of *The Presbyterian Hymnal* (1990) will find this structure in *Glory to God* as well, but within the broader framework of God's gracious acts: Advent coincides with anticipations of the messiah; Christmas, with Jesus' birth; and so on. Those accustomed to looking for the Psalms in one central section, as they appeared in 1990, will instead find them within their respective salvation-story themes (Psalm 8, "O Lord, Our God, How Excellent" [#25], is in the section titled "Creation and Providence"; Psalm 19, "Your Law, O Lord, Is Perfect" [#61], in the section on Covenant; Psalm 72, "All Hail to God's Anointed" [#149], in the celebration of Christ's birth). A specific psalm listing within the scriptural index at the back of the book facilitates the search for individual psalms.

Because God has shown us such grace through salvation history, we respond with gratitude. This response begins as we come together to learn what God has done; hence, the service music of "The Church at Worship" forms the central section of the book. Following it are hymns expressing our adoration and dedication to the One "to whom our lives belong."

In *Glory to God* we profess our faith in this God not only through a variety of sung forms but also through spoken liturgy. The book contains roughly thirty pages outlining orders of service for the Lord's Day (including the celebration of the

Lord's Supper); for baptism; for morning, evening, and night prayers; and a collection of other texts for use in worship such as the Nicene Creed, the Apostles' Creed, the Ten Commandments, and A Brief Statement of Faith.

What, then, is this book? Robed in purple or deep red, it is a treasure trove of biblical study, church history, poetry, music, and theology, offering up riches to shape the faith and life of God's people for generations to come.

"DO NOT NEGLECT TO SHOW HOSPITALITY" (HEB. 13:2)

How can we best introduce this treasure trove to others? First off, we should remember that leaders facilitating the transition to a new hymnal do not need to persuade the *early adopters* (whose enthusiasm is already likely to have fueled the vote to purchase new materials); nor do we need to convert the *never adopters* (who are still wondering why the *last* hymnal was put in the pews). Rather, our challenge is to appeal to those *middle adopters* who, as a reasonable habit, will question any change before endorsing it personally.

The following paragraphs offer specific suggestions for introducing a new hymnal to this group—and, coincidentally, to the rest of a congregation. The guiding metaphor is one of hospitality. How would we go about introducing a visiting friend to our home congregation so that she and they might form the best first impression of one other? We would probably not begin by reciting her entire history, listing all her degrees and accomplishments, friends, and relations. "Too much information," as the current colloquialism puts it, constitutes a barrier rather than a bridge to communication. Rather, we would focus on a few points of interest likely to establish common ground: "This is my friend Sarah; she's a Buckeye fan," or "she goes fly-fishing on weekends," or "she used to volunteer one night a month at the homeless shelter of her inner-city congregation."

But too little information is also a barrier to building relationships. In using the metaphor of hospitality, I am assuming that we truly want our congregation to welcome the new hymnal as they would welcome a new friend or prospective new member. This means that we cannot simply have the book show up in the pew racks on a given Sunday, unanticipated and unannounced, and expect a response other than resistance from the middle adopter majority. A thoughtful process of preparation is crucial. A countdown, like an Advent calendar, can help prepare the way. "Quick Facts" in the church newsletter, on the church website, or on a church bulletin board can serve a function analogous to the well-crafted introduction of a visitor.

> We truly want our congregation to welcome the new hymnal as they would welcome a new friend.

Information to share in an introduction to the new hymnal should consist of facts that are interesting to your own congregation. For example, does your congregation have members who come from a Dutch-reformed tradition? Let them know about Dutch tunes and translated Dutch texts in *Glory to God* (like Huub Oosterhuis's "What Is This Place"). Do your members enjoy gospel songs? Be sure to tell them that "I Love to Tell the Story," "Leaning on the Everlasting Arms," and "Shall We Gather at the River" are part of the new hymnal. Do you have an African drumming group, or would you like to form one? Highlight the wealth of songs from Africa that you will soon be able to sing together to lively rhythmic accompaniment. Do you have a partner church in a Latin American country? Look at the number of Spanish-language hymns you can learn to sing in both English and Spanish for your next visit with them. Is Bible study an important part of your Christian nurture program for children, youth, and adults? Let people know that every book in the Bible (even Obadiah and Philemon!) is referenced in at least one hymn or song and that hymns average over six biblical references apiece.

Hard as it may be for innovator and early adopter types to restrain their enthusiasm, we need not rush to begin using the new hymnal church-wide the minute a shipment of boxes arrives from the publisher. Think again of that visiting friend: would you introduce her to the whole congregation at once, or might you instead take her to a smaller group gathered at the coffee hour, or in a learning hour class, and make initial introductions there? Extending the analogy, think about what groups in your congregation might be best suited to make an early acquaintance with the new hymnal. People respond more favorably to change if they have a role to play in the process. So, what individuals from the cautiously inquisitive, middle adopter group might you enlist to study the new hymnal and help teach others about it?

"SEEK AND YOU WILL FIND" (MATT. 7:7)

This series of lessons provides one possible starting point for such a study. If you think your congregation would prefer a more informal way to engage with these questions than an organized learning hour, you might send a select group of people off with copies of the new hymnal and instructions to conduct a sort of scavenger hunt for answers to the following questions (and possibly generating further questions and answers of their own).

1. Did you know some hymns in the former hymnal so well that you even knew what *number* they were? Check

to see if your "number-known" hymns are still present in *Glory to God*. Since more than 65 percent of the former hymnal carried forward, the odds are good that they will be. What are their *new* numbers?

2. Look for hymns that appear in *Glory to God* in more than one language. Where does the English text appear on the page relative to the music? Is this the same or different from other hymnals?

3. Look for hymns with five stanzas. "The Church's One Foundation" is one example; "I Greet Thee, Who My Sure Redeemer Art" is another. Where does the fifth stanza appear on the page in relation to the lines of music? How does this compare with other hymnals? What about hymns with six stanzas (for example, "Our God, Our Help in Ages Past")?

4. Have you ever participated in a Taizé worship service? What pieces of music can you find that are attributed to Jacques Berthier or the Taizé Community?

5. Have any members of your church ever visited the island of Iona off the coast of Scotland? What songs can you find attributed to John Bell and Graham Maule or the Iona Community?

6. One of the most popular "new" songs from the 1990 hymnal is "Here I Am, Lord." Is anything else by the same author in *Glory to God*? Another popular one from the 1990 hymnal is "God of the Sparrow," with words by Jaroslav Vajda and music by Carl Schalk. What pieces have they contributed, together or separately, to the 2013 collection? (Note: Authors and composers appear in a single index in the back of *Glory to God*, whereas some other hymnals contain separate indexes for authors/translators and composers/arrangers.)

7. Who are the authors or composers responsible for your personal favorite hymns (whether you recall their hymn

numbers or not)? How well represented are these writers in the new hymnal? What do you learn about them and their works from the accompanying program notes?
8. Not all Advent hymns are located in *Glory to God* in the section just before carols celebrating the birth of Jesus. Some, like "Sleepers, Wake!" and "Lo, He Comes with Clouds Descending" appear in a much later section. Why?
9. How many hymns appear in the baptism section of *Glory to God*? How many in the section devoted to the Lord's Supper? How does this compare with other hymnals?
10. Generally speaking, when a hymn or song appears in *Glory to God* in a language with a non-Roman alphabet (e.g. Korean or Mandarin Chinese), how is the other language rendered? Contrast, for example, the appearance of "Lonely the Boat" in *Glory to God* and some other hymnal.

In the process of seeking answers to these questions, people will independently discover a number of key ways in which *Glory to God* differs from its predecessors. Provide opportunities for such findings to be shared, inviting speculation about why the Presbyterian Committee on Congregational Song made the choices it did in these areas. Such experiential and analytical learning will help people "befriend" the new hymnal far better than simply placing it in the pews and expecting them to sing out of it without the benefit of further introduction.

MAKE NEW FRIENDS, BUT . . .

Once the hymnal *is* in the pew racks, the process of introducing it to the full congregation must still move with appropriate caution—like porcupines passing the peace. Some congregations will be more accustomed than others to trying new music; some will have already encountered many of the new songs from *Glory to God* through their work as test sites during the process of hymnal creation or through their use of the 2011 and 2012 samplers. Some worship planners have for years taken weekly advantage of their church's copyright license to create bulletin inserts that incorporate materials not in the congregation's pew hymnal. Some congregations do not use a print volume at all but regularly download new material to project onto a screen.

Churches thus function along a continuum of comfort with novelty: from "eagerly explores new material at every service, never singing the same thing twice" to "engages in threats of membership withdrawal and non-payment of pledges if anything beyond a familiar twenty songs is ever attempted." Most congregations exist somewhere between these extremes. As noted in chapter 2, people resist change not so much from lack of vision as from fear of loss. They need reassurance that the old hymns that have been so important in their journeys of faith have not disappeared. Making new friends is much easier when we are confident that we may also keep the old.

A wise worship planner, therefore, will resist the temptation to do too many new things too fast. Many of a congregation's old favorite hymns are likely to be included in *Glory to God* since the selection of materials for the collection was informed by survey data about what people found most meaningful to sing. If you do not actually know what your congregation's favorite hymns are, now would be the perfect time to find out with a survey in the church newsletter or a suggestion box in the narthex. Find those hymns in the new hymnal and *use them*.

And take a tip from John Calvin. When his colleagues Clément Marot and Louis Bourgeois had composed a new metric psalm for his congregation in Geneva, he had them first teach it to the children. *Glory to God* is filled with simple, engaging songs from all over the world that a children's choir or Sunday school class could easily learn. If the children lead, the adults will follow, exploring together the riches in our new musical treasure trove.

> Sing new songs, but keep the old:
> one is silver, and the other, gold.

Appendix 1

FIFTEEN FACTS ABOUT *GLORY TO GOD*

1. The most frequently asked question about the new hymnal prior to its publication was, What color will it be? After extensive marketing research, the Presbyterian Publishing Corporation decided to offer the hymnal in two colors: purple and red. For an additional fee, a name can be embossed on the front of the hymnal, in silver for purple editions or in gold for red ones. *Glory to God* is also available in an ecumenical edition: same colors and contents but without the PC(USA) name and seal.
2. The second most frequent prepublication question was, How much will it weigh? *Glory to God* weighs 2 pounds, 3.5 ounces, making it slightly lighter (and thinner) than the 1990 hymnal. It will fit easily into existing pew racks!
3. Hymns and songs written to be sung in unison appear in the pew edition of the hymnal with just the singing part printed (the melody line, without the musical staffs underneath for piano or organ accompaniment); however, most of these

have chord symbols that guitar or keyboard players can use. (Where no chord symbols are included, it is because the music comes out of a tradition that does not use chordal accompaniment.) Still, roughly two-thirds of the hymns in the book appear in four-part harmony. By printing traditional unison hymns without accompaniment, we were able to create a collection of 853 pieces that weighs less than the former hymnal, which contains 605.

4. Before arriving at its final selection of 853 hymns, psalms, and spiritual songs, the Presbyterian Committee on Congregational Song reviewed some ten thousand texts and pieces of music. This means that only 8.53 percent of the materials reviewed were chosen for inclusion (which also means that any pieces not selected for inclusion are in very good company with the remaining 91.47 percent!).

5. All materials reviewed for inclusion were considered anonymously (with names of authors, composers, and copyright holders removed) so that votes could be based solely on the merits of the pieces or their ability to fill identified gaps in the repertoire.

6. The hymn from the 1990 hymnal about which the Presbyterian Committee on Congregational Song received the most mail was "Be Thou My Vision." In response to numerous critiques and requests, we returned the language of the hymn closer to the version that appeared in the 1955 *Hymnbook*.

7. The text subgroup of the hymnal committee did extensive research so that the words of hymns more often reflect versions being used by our ecumenical partners. Even though as Christians we have divided ourselves into different denominations, we can still sing the same words to the same songs!

8. Because singing the Psalms holds such a central place in the history of the Reformed tradition, *Glory to God* includes full settings of 106 of the 150 psalms (see the Psalm Index, pp.

989–990). These psalm settings reflect a diversity of musical genres, from the Genevan and Scottish Psalters to global and contemporary praise and worship arrangements, and a handful of responsive readings. Literally hundreds more references or allusions to lines from the psalms appear in the book. (See the Scriptural Index, pp. 979–988.)

9. In addition to the Psalms, every book of the Bible is referenced in at least one hymn. More than 2,200 references appear to texts from the Old Testament, and there are more than 3,200 references to texts from the New. Testament

10. *Glory to God* also contains a Lectionary Index (pp. 968–978) to assist worship planners with multiple hymn recommendations for every Sunday of the three-year common lectionary.

11. Music from churches in Africa, Latin America, and the Middle East is amply reflected in the book, as is a wide representation of songs from Asia (especially from places like Korea and Taiwan, where the Presbyterian Church is strong). But in most instances, the English words appear directly under the music, with words from the other languages farther down the page. Below is a representative (but in no way exhaustive) sampling, from A to Z:

    Arab Christians: "Holy Lamb of God" (#602)
    Argentina: "This Is the Day" (#391)
    Brazil: "For the Troubles and the Sufferings" (#764)
    Cameroon: "He Came Down" (#137)
    Caribbean: "The Right Hand of God" (#332)
    China: "Golden Breaks the Dawn" (#668)
    Cuba: "The Lord Now Sends Us Forth" (#747)

Democratic Republic of Congo:	"Know That God Is Good" (#659)
Dominican Republic:	"Alleluia! Christ Is Arisen" (#253)
Ghana:	"Praise God, All You Nations" (#328)
India:	"Give Us Light" (#467)
Israel:	"Come and Sing the Praise of the Lord" (#389)
Kenya:	"Listen, God Is Calling" (#456)
Korea:	"Dream On, Dream On" (#383)
Liberia:	"Come, Let Us Eat" (#528)
Maori (New Zealand):	"Son of God, Whose Heart Is Peace" (#425)
Nigeria:	"Come, O Holy Spirit, Come" (#283)
Pakistan:	"Blest Be God, Praised Forever" (#617)
Philippines:	"In the Heavens Shone a Star" (#131)
Rwanda:	"Heaven Opened to Isaiah" (#68)
Singapore:	"As the Wind Song" (#292)
South Africa:	"Amen, We Praise Your Name" (#598)
Swaziland:	"We Will Walk with God" (#742)
Taiwan:	"Let Us Come to Worship God" (#387)
Tanzania:	"Christ Has Arisen, Alleluia" (#251)
Zimbabwe:	"Come All You People" (#388)

12. A number of the most respected songwriters of the contemporary worship movement are represented, people like Paul Baloche, Michael Joncas, Graham Kendrick, Rich Mullins, Martin Nystrom, Twila Paris, Martin Smith, Michael Smith, and Chris Tomlin.
13. Even more gospel songs and African American spirituals than in the 1990 hymnal are included, such as:

"Just a Closer Walk with Thee" (#835)
"Keep Your Lamps Trimmed and Burning" (#350)
"Lead Me, Guide Me" (#740)
"Steal Away" (#358)
"Swing Low, Sweet Chariot" (#825)

14. More than 65 percent of the blue 1990 hymnal is carrying forward, from old standards to newer favorites like "God of the Sparrow" (#22); "Here I Am, Lord" (#69); "I Danced in the Morning" (#157); "Lift High the Cross" (#826); and "Lord, You Have Come to the Lakeshore" (#721). The majority of the hymns from the blue hymnal not chosen for use in *Glory to God* include pieces that had not been widely used by congregations around the country—certain settings of the Psalms, pieces of service music, late twentieth-century texts, and global songs—so different examples in each of these categories were sought.
15. A number of old favorites from the 1955 "red hymnal" are making a comeback, including such beloved heart songs as:

"Be Still, My Soul" (#819)
"I Heard the Voice of Jesus Say" (#182)
"I Love to Tell the Story" (#462)
"I Need Thee Every Hour" (#735)
"Jesus Calls Us" (#720)
"Judge Eternal, Throned in Splendor" (#342)
"Rock of Ages, Cleft for Me" (#438)
"Sometimes a Light Surprises" (#800)

And there are also some "golden oldies" *never* or *rarely* seen before in a Presbyterian hymnal:

> "His Eye Is on the Sparrow" / "Why Should I Feel Discouraged? (#661)
> "It Is Well with My Soul" / "When Peace like a River" (#840)
> "Leaning on the Everlasting Arms" / "What a Fellowship, What a Joy Divine" (#837)
> "Shall We Gather at the River" (#375) (only in the 1874 edition)
> "Softly and Tenderly Jesus Is Calling" (#418)
> "Standing on the Promises" (#838)

Appendix 2

SUGGESTED USES FOR OLD HYMNALS

Offer the existing hymnal a dignified and respectful retirement, perhaps with a specific liturgy of thanksgiving on the Sunday before you introduce the new collection. Celebrate the gifts it has brought to your congregation's worship, and find ways that it can still be of use even if it is no longer "employed" full-time.

Keep enough copies in the choir room so that a summer pick-up ensemble can sing occasional anthems out of it. Place copies in all spaces of the church where groups are likely to gather: Sunday school classrooms, the fellowship hall, the session meeting room, the Scout hut. Having hymnals available in all these places should make it easier to incorporate hymns on a regular basis into the Christian nurture of your congregation.

Check with a local religious-affiliated retirement community to see if they would like hymnals to put in bedside tables in their assisted living facility.

When a natural disaster strikes—flood, earthquake, fire—see if there is a church whose hymnals have been damaged or destroyed who would appreciate receiving the gift of your still eminently useful "retirees."

In some parts of the country, historic churches are being restored for occasional use; a gift of gently-sung-from books enables such places to serve not just as museums but as places where people can again sing together in prayer and praise.

If copies bear bookplates from having been donated in memory of or in honor of particular individuals, offer people with remaining ties to the honorees an opportunity to take the dedicated copies for their own use or to give them to other friends and relatives.

Encourage any members of the congregation who do not already have hymnals at home to take a copy of the former book to keep at a bedside table for morning or evening devotions or near a musical instrument for sight-reading practice.

If a member is moving away from the church, send her or him off with a keepsake copy of the "old" hymnal, inscribed by other members with words of support and encouragement on pages bearing their personal favorite hymns. Do the same for any young person going away to college or for confirmands entering into a new relationship with their church family.

If the bindings of the former hymnals show significant signs of wear, use a razor blade to remove individual pages and mail them, with a handwritten message, as greeting cards: seasonal hymns for seasons' greetings; hymns of comfort and reassurance as condolences; the hymns of a particular Sunday's service with a note such as, "We sang this last week and thought of you." Deacons could think of further creative ways to extend the ministry of books that still have significant life in them even if their full-time use is being superseded by a more recent collection.

www.ingramcontent.com/pod-product-compliance
Lightning Source LLC
Chambersburg PA
CBHW072055290426

44110CB00014B/1696